y Journal.

ARY 29. 1728.

ails from Flanders.
The general Di-
Fishery, being in
ose last Year, a
eir Order, to St.
ertain Number of
the Service of next

Captain Ramsey,
in the Charles, in
acusa, and in 22
on the 26th past,
Gatt and Cartha-
, Captain William
ne, both from St.
and; and on the
20 Leagues West
's, with the ——
ohn Higgs, from
nd to Alicant.
is Majesty's Ship
the Downs Yester-
y's Ship Dolphin,
the Stamboline,
or Smyrna; the
horogood, for Lis-
ptain Willis, the
and the Pleasant,
Oporto; and the
wall, for St. Chri-
ortune for Havre.
nd *sailed* thro' the
kenden, for Barba-
d the Pelican, Cap-
alaga; and this
ver, Captain Ma-
-York, for Amster-
Beaver, Captain

Saturday last South-Sea Stock was 108 1 8th, 108 3 8ths, 108 1 8th. South-Sea Annuity 104 1 half, 104 3 8ths, 104 1 half, 104 5 8ths. India 169 1 half. Three per Cent. Annuity 87, to 87 1 4th. Bank 136 3 4ths, 136 1 half. York-Buildings 11 1 4th to 11 1 half. Royal Assurance 93 to 94. London Assurance 13 1 8th. African 54. India Bonds 3 l. 12 s. Prem. South-Sea Bonds 5 l. 5 s. Prem.

Never Acted before,
By the Company of COMEDIANS,

AT the Theatre-Royal in Lincoln's-Inn Fields, this present Monday, being the 29th Day of January, will be presented, The BEGGAR's OPERA. Boxes 5s. Pit 3s. Gallery 2s.

SIR, *London, Jan. 27.*

THE Office of Chamberlain of this City being vacant by the Death of Sir GEORGE LUDLAM, at the earnest Request of many eminent Citizens,

Lieut. Coll. SAMUEL ROBINSON,
Citizen and Joyner,

Stands Candidate for the said Office, and humbly desires the Favour and Friendship of the Worthy Gentlemen of the Livery, to support his Interest on this Occasion.

N. B. The Day of Election being appointed for Tuesday the 6th of February next, and my only Dependance being on the Free and Voluntary Votes of my Fellow-Citizens (a Dependance more Noble in itself, than any other whatsoever) I heartily intreat not only the Continuance of the Application of my Friends, but more particularly that they would be pleased to give their early Appearance in the Hall on the Morning of the Election.

To the Worthy Liverymen of LONDON.
Gentlemen,

BEing advised by my Friends to decline standing at this Juncture, for Chamberlain of this Honourable City, I return most

LIVING IN ENGLAND

FIELDING'S ENGLAND

The Endpapers

ont. Until 1751 New Year's Day was officially March 1st in England; ut since 1600 it had been January 1st in Scotland and that day was ften used unofficially in England. Thus when you read eighteenth entury documents dated in the months of January, February or March, is not always certain which year they refer to. This newspaper uses he 'new style' in its heading. It was published in the first month of 728; but in column one a correspondent has used the 'old style'. He iinks of January as the tenth month of the year 1727.

The Daily Journal
Monday, January 29, 1728
South-Sea House, Jan 27, 1727

Letter-writers often put both years, like this one who wrote on what we would call March 10th, 1736, but what some people still hought of as the 10th day of the twelfth month of 1735.

ly dearest London, March 10th, $\frac{1735}{6}$

In this book January is taken as the first month of the year. This the usual practice even when writing about the years before 1751. A further difficulty is that before 1752 the English calendar was eleven ays behind the correct one used on the continent; but in a book like iis, in which no foreign documents are quoted, no confusion arises.

Back. Map of London engraved in 1725.

The Jacket

The jacket shows details of embroidered panels which can be seen at Montacute House, Somerset. They were worked on canvas in wool and silk during the early eighteenth century. A party of four are shown having a meal. One of the footmen serving them has tripped and fallen, perhaps frightened by the dog or the monkey. Additional entertainment is provided by a harpist.

A lady and gentleman of about 1730. He is 19½ inches tall and wears a brown coat. She is 17 inches tall and wears a white muslin dress over a corset. Both are dolls. Their heads and bodies are wooden. Their eyes are glass.

LIVING IN ENGLAND

FIELDING'S ENGLAND

DUNCAN TAYLOR

London
DENNIS DOBSON

By the same author

Living in England: Chaucer's England

Living in England: The Elizabethan Age

IN MEMORY OF H.J.T.

'Woman not inferior to man'

First published in Great Britain in 1966
by Dobson Books Ltd, 80 Kensington Church Street,
London, W.8

Printed in Great Britain by
Butler & Tanner Ltd, Frome and London

CONTENTS

Fielding's tomb in Lisbon.

ACKNOWLEDGEMENTS

Acknowledgement is made to the following for permission to reproduce pictures on the pages listed:

The Trustees of the British Museum: *pages* 8, 16, 17, 50, 64–66, 70, 75 and endpapers 103, 149, 170, 176, 210, 227, 233
Cambridge University Press (*An Historical Geography of England before 1800* ed. H. C. Darby): *pages* 29, 37
Chatto & Windus Ltd (*Social Life in the Reign of Queen Anne*): *pages* 194, 223, 229, 247
The Thomas Coram Foundation for Children: *pages* 33, 91, 125, 184
Country Life: *page* 55
Coutts & Co: *page* 164
Coventry City Council: *pages* 96, 139, 160, 231
General Electric Company Ltd: *page* 25
His Grace the Duke of Marlborough: *page* 54
Imperial Tobacco Co: *page* 204–205
The Trustees of Dr Johnson's House: *page* 209
King's College, Cambridge: *page* 106
Dr Sylvia Lawler: *page* 5
The Trustees of the London Museum: *pages* 19, 30, 57, 80, 197, 198, 220
Longmans Green & Co Ltd: *pages* 39, 151
The Lord Chamberlain's Office (Crown Copyright): *pages* 27, 58
Martins Bank Ltd: *page* 165
Middlesex County Council: *page* 62
Ministry of Defence (R.A.F.) (Crown Copyright): *pages* 118, 126, 127
The Trustees of the National Portrait Gallery: *pages* 92, 121, 133, 155, 199, 201
Photo Precision: *page* 56
The Postmaster General: *page* 41
The Royal College of Surgeons: *page* 143
Science Museum, London (Crown Copyright): *pages* 237, 243
Sheffield City Libraries: *page* 100
Sheffield City Museum: *page* 163
The Trustees of Sir John Soane's Museum: *pages* 36, 111, 203, 246, 250
The Society of Friends: *page* 131
Sotheby & Co: *pages* 67, 78, 82, 108
The Times: *pages* 60, 146, 157, 191, 218, 219, 228
The Trustees of the Victoria & Albert Museum: *pages* 2, 63, 77, 84, 87, 104, 169
The Wardens of Spanish and Portuguese Jews' Congregation, and Judges Ltd: *page* 136
Wellcome Historical Medical Museum: *pages* 89, 141
Woodfall Films and United Artists: *pages* 10, 14, 45, 47, 48, 94, 174, 187

Every effort has been made to trace the ownership of all illustrative material used in this book. Should any error in acknowledgement have been made the Publishers offer their apologies and will be glad to make the necessary correction in future editions.

INTRODUCTION

EIGHTEENTH-CENTURY books often began with a dedication to the patron who had kept the author from starvation while he was writing. This dedication had to be long and fulsome. It would never have done to dedicate, as P. G. Wodehouse once did: 'To My Daughter LEONORA without whose never-failing sympathy and encouragement this book would have been finished in half the time.' Irony was well understood in the eighteenth century, but the dedication was no place for it. The accepted form was to say that you knew My Lord could not abide compliments and then to lay such compliments on with a trowel. Thus:

And here, if I were able duly to celebrate your own accomplishments and perfections, I should willingly attempt it; but that I know you would be displeased at anything that carrieth the face of a panegyrick, though it had never so much truth in it. All, therefore, all that I dare venture upon, is, but just to hint, in a transient manner, at your innate sweetness of temper, and honourable (though now-a-days unfashionable) sincerity and probity; which, together with your many other rare virtues and endowments, render you admired, honoured, and beloved, by all that have had the happiness to know you: and in a particular manner by, My Lord, your Lordship's most obliged, most devoted, and faithful servant, T. Fuller.

Fuller was a doctor, but even Fielding, who was a professional humorist, could not avoid beginning *Tom Jones* with a serious dedication. It goes on for pages and concludes with the author more or less on bended knee:

Pardon what I have said in this epistle . . . and give me at least leave, in this public manner, to declare that I am, with the highest respect and gratitude,—

Sir,

Your most obliged,

Obedient, humble servant,

HENRY FIELDING.

The person addressed was in fact an old friend. Fielding had been at Eton with him. But convention demanded a dedication dripping with flattery and self-abasement.

I have not followed this convention. I would, however, like to take one short extract from the dedication to *Tom Jones* and make the same two requests of the reader that Fielding makes:

> First, that he [the reader] will not expect to find perfection in this work; and secondly, that he will excuse some parts of it, if they fall short of that little merit which I hope may appear in others.

Henry Fielding in his forty-eighth year (the year of his death), by Hogarth. The masks commemorate his plays; behind them are some of his novels, including *Tom Jones.* The sword and scales and the book entitled *Statutes* commemorate his work as a magistrate.

Henry Fielding

Henry Fielding was born in Somerset during the reign of Queen Anne (1707). His father was a country gentleman, who, it seems, could afford Eton, where Fielding went in 1720, but not the Grand Tour of Europe, sometimes lasting several years, with which young gentlemen then completed their education. Nor did Fielding go to Cambridge or Oxford. Instead he began to write plays. The first was produced at Drury Lane in 1728, before Fielding was 21.

Fielding next went to the University of Leyden in Holland, but was back in London by 1730, when his second play was produced. Other plays followed—comedies, farces, adaptations from the French; but none of them was a spectacular success. Fielding did not make much money; but his wife, whom he married in 1734, inherited some and they were able to spend a year in Dorset, after which he returned to London, took the Little Theatre in the Haymarket and formed a company of actors (1736). But the first two plays which Fielding provided for them were so daringly satirical, particularly in reference to politicians, that Sir Robert Walpole, the Prime Minister, introduced into Parliament a theatrical licensing act which tightened the control of the Lord Chamberlain over all theatrical performances.

The Lord Chamberlain still has the power to censor stage plays. Some writers find his authority irksome; but they do not stop writing plays because of it. Fielding did. He began to write novels instead.

Daniel Defoe (1659-1731), author of *Robinson Crusoe* and *Moll Flanders*, is generally regarded as the founder of the English novel. After him came Samuel Richardson (1689-1761), a printer, who had reached the age of fifty without writing anything noteworthy, and became suddenly famous when he wrote *Pamela* (1740). Fielding's first novel, *Joseph Andrews,* followed in 1742. Smollett (1721-1771), a Scot who had been a surgeon in the navy and had written a play which no manager would accept, succeeded in 1748 with the novel *Roderick Random.* This was followed the next year by Fielding's *Tom Jones.*

Albert Finney as Tom Jones.

Novel-writing was only an incident in Fielding's life and, though it brought him more money than his plays, it did not make him rich. He had meanwhile been reading for the bar and had practised as a barrister. In

1744 his wife died. Next year the 'forty-five' rebellion led him to turn to journalism. He founded a paper called *The True Patriot* (Fielding was no Jacobite). In 1747 he married his wife's maid. Next year he was made a magistrate for Middlesex and Westminster. The post brought him £300 a year and a house in Bow Street, where there is still a magistrate's court. But it meant hard work. A magistrate today has only to try criminals. Fielding was also concerned with catching them, since there was no regular police force in the eighteenth century. At the same time he managed to go on with his writing, but not for long. His health broke down. In June 1754 he sailed with his wife and eldest daughter to Lisbon, where he hoped the warmer climate might make him better. But it did not. He arrived in August and in October he died, at the age of 47—a man who admired generosity and kindliness, loathed humbug and loved his wives.

Fielding's England

Fielding lived during the reigns of Anne (1702-1714), George I (1714-1727) and George II (1727-1760), which together make up the approximate period covered by this book. His novels, in particular *Joseph Andrews* and *Tom Jones*, have contributed much to it. So the book bears his name.

'Fielding's England' is also to some extent 'Defoe's England'. Daniel Defoe was nearly fifty when Fielding was born, so that their lifetimes do not overlap closely. But in 1724 Defoe published *A Tour through England and Wales* and any book on the first half of the eighteenth century is likely to use the *Tour* as a source. Defoe, one of the earliest writers who can be called a 'journalist', wrote much that is of interest to anyone asking the question: How did people live then? Some of his fiction is as useful as his reporting. *Robinson Crusoe,* which

everyone has heard of and few have read, has obvious limitations as a source book for English home life; but *Moll Flanders* is more helpful. Nobody knows how much it mixes fact with fiction, but there is no doubt that the background provides an authentic picture of England at the period when the book was first published (1722). More will therefore be heard of Moll, and also of another fictitious character, Sir Roger de Coverley, whom Sir Richard Steele (1672-1729) brought to life in a periodical called *The Spectator*.

What about Dr. Johnson (1709-1784)? He was only two years younger than Fielding, but it was not till the second half of the century that he reached his greatest fame. The years 1740-1780 are called 'Johnson's England' in G. M. Trevelyan's *English Social History* and elsewhere. To this period belong, for example, the actor, Garrick; the painters, Reynolds and Gainsborough; the writers, Goldsmith and Gibbon; and, in part, the Methodists, John and Charles Wesley. Johnson's England needs a book to itself.*

* E.g. *Johnson's England*, Edited by A. S. Turbeville, 2 Vols. with 158 illustrations, Clarendon Press 1933.

'Living in England'

History is like ham, in so far as it is sometimes sliced horizontally, into periods, and sometimes vertically, into subjects. Having defined our period as approximately the first half of the eighteenth century, it remains to define the subject. Like previous books in the series—*Chaucer's England* and *The Elizabethan Age*—this one tries both to provide a picture of life in England at a certain period and to point to things—e.g. houses, furniture or books—which still survive from that period. Like its predecessors, *Fielding's England* aims at being a travel book and a guide book, to a period instead of to a country. These two aims are not always easy to reconcile. A travel book must be readable; a guide is primarily for reference. In this series, readability comes first, but it is hoped that the index will make the book useful for reference, e.g. for finding the answer to a given question, for getting details right in the production of a period play, or for planning sightseeing.

There are a great many dates. Those who do not want them can skip them, but they have their uses. Our period is a long one. It might be convenient if we took one moment—say midday on January 29th, 1728, when *The Beggar's Opera* had its first night—and described England as it was then. But it would be very difficult and it would also be very dull. A wider expanse of time is needed if you want plenty of characters and events to choose from. So having chosen an expanse of fifty years, one must be precise within that period. Building was going on; fashions were changing; laws were being passed. What is true of 1707 may not necessarily be true of 1745.

It is therefore useful to date events. It is also useful to give the dates of people, when they are first mentioned. You can then tell what age they were in any year and this helps to form a picture of what they may have looked like.

Although there are a great many dates, there are not many references to what battles were fought and what laws were passed in Parliament. This is not because such history is unimportant. The reason is simply that such subjects are thoroughly dealt with in other books and frequently studied in school. I assume that many readers of this book will already know something of the victories won by the Duke of Marlborough (1650-1722), of Sir Robert Walpole (1676-1745), the first Prime Minister, and of the difference between a Whig and a Tory. Such matters, to return to our metaphor, are a different slice of ham.

'Bon appetit.'

Hugh Griffith as Squire Western.

CHAPTER I

LONDON AND ENGLAND

The West End in 1745

TOM JONES, the handsome, brave, generous and affectionate hero of Fielding's most famous novel, rode into London from the north, through St. Albans and Barnet.

Today Barnet is one of the places where London begins. Loneliness, at that point in his journey, is the least of a traveller's worries. But Barnet in the year 1745, when Jones rode through with his servant, was a village. To the south the rough road passed between cultivated fields and then plunged into woods as it mounted Highgate Hill.

These woods were dangerous. They sheltered highwaymen. Sure enough, Jones was held up. But the pistol which was poked into his ribs turned out to be unloaded. The man who held it was not a regular highwayman, but a bungling amateur who had only recently turned robber in order to provide for his six children. Jones, characteristically, forgave the man and presented him with two guineas. Jones's servant thought that he should have been hanged.

From the top of Highgate Hill the travellers could have seen St. Paul's, as we can now. The last and highest stone of the dome had been ceremonially laid in 1710. But evening was coming on and Jones had not come to London to see the sights. He was trying to find

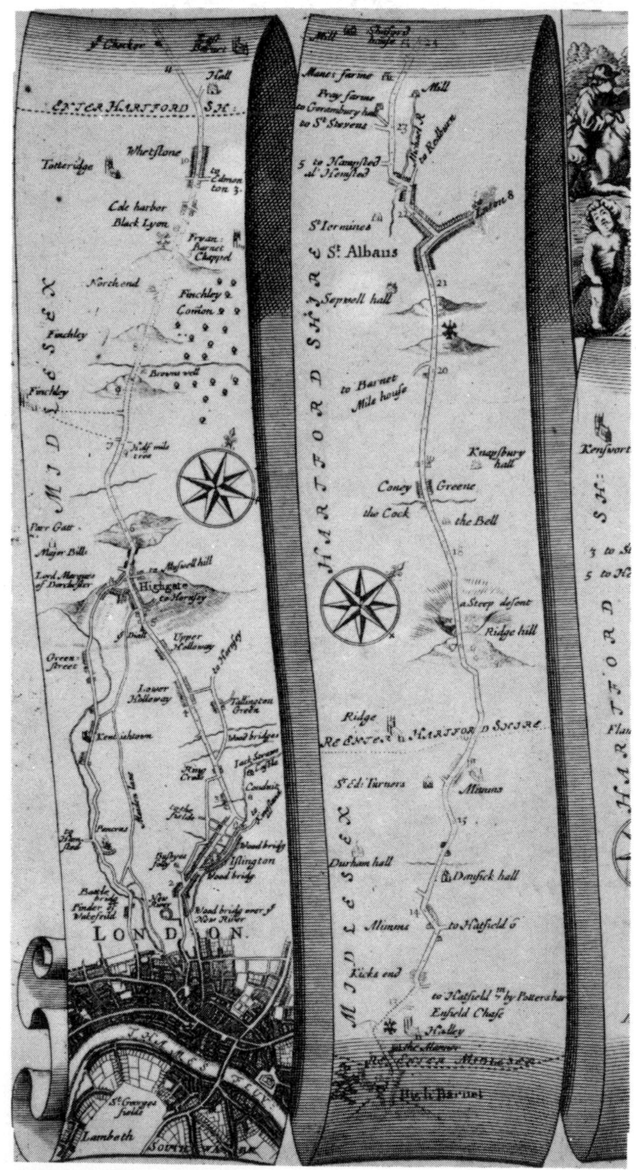

From John Ogilby's map of Middlesex, *c.* 1677.

Oxford Street and Cavendish Square, 1745. Oxford Circus ⊗.

a girl called Sophia Western, whom he had loved for a long time in Gloucestershire. She had black hair, curled at the level of her neck, and arched eyebrows. It was of her that Jones was thinking as he entered the built-up area of London near where King's Cross Station now stands and ended his journey in Holborn, at the Bull and Gate Inn.

Sophia had arrived in London in the coach and six of an Irish nobleman. Jones knew this, but he did not know where the nobleman lived. Where should he begin his search? Not in the City of London; a lord would not have lived there in 1745, nor along the Strand, where dukes had once built palaces with gateways on to the Thames. No. Tom Jones, looking for a lord in London two hundred years ago, looked where you or I might look today, in the fashionable districts which the Post Office has labelled S.W.1.. and W.1. and which in Jones's time were comparatively new.

In the west London squares (which, by the way, are not always square) most of the houses belonged to titled people. St. James's, the oldest of the squares, where building had begun in the reign of Charles II, housed four dukes and seven earls by 1726; Grosvenor Square, dating from the 1720's, had fifteen earls, two dowager duchesses and a duke about the time when Tom Jones made his search; Hanover Square (built 1716-1720), Cavendish Square (begun in 1717), Berkeley Square (begun in 1698) and the neighbouring streets would also have been worth combing for a vanished nobleman. But it was no good going further west or north. At that time this district of handsome squares lay on the edge of London. Beyond it were fields. Fortunately Tom Jones heard news of Sophia and her black curls before he wandered so far.

St. James's, Westminster and Whitehall

Two splendid residences in this aristocratic neighbourhood—St. James's Palace and Marlborough House—were not on any of the famous squares.

Wren had begun Marlborough House for the Duke of Marlborough in the year of his last great victory (Malplaquet, 1709), and since the destruction of Whitehall Palace by fire in 1698, St. James's had been the royal residence nearest to Westminster. William and Mary had liked living in the new palace which Wren had built for them at Kensington. So had Anne. But the Georges had brought the Court back to St. James's. Not far away the Duke of Buckingham had built himself a mansion which George III later turned into Buckingham Palace.

Westminster Hall remained unchanged, but there were many later buildings near it. The Abbey had been provided with two new western towers designed by Nicholas Hawksmoor (1740); Inigo Jones's banqueting hall (1622)

Westminster Hall, 1738. Law Courts at far end and left foreground. Booksellers and milliners at sides. The Law Courts were at Westminster until 1882.

had survived the fire which destroyed Whitehall Palace; Admiralty House had been completed in 1722 (the Horse Guards rose next to it in 1753). Some inconspicuous but elegant houses had appeared in Queen Anne's Gate and in Downing Street.

No. 10 Downing Street

Though inconspicuous, Downing Street was to become famous. It had begun as a property speculation made by George Downing in the seventeenth century. Born in Ireland and educated at Harvard, Downing was sufficiently astute to please both sides in the Civil War. Cromwell made him an ambassador. Charles II made him a knight.

The first owner of No. 10 Downing Street was a nobleman less adept than Downing at adjusting his loyalties to the changing times; so when James II left England,

The orangery, Kensington Palace.

Porch and torch extinguisher, 26 Queen Anne's Gate.

this nobleman left with him. No. 10 was forfeited and became royal property. In 1731 George II offered it as a present to Sir Robert Walpole, the first Prime Minister. Walpole refused and it was agreed that the house should go with the office of Prime Minister, which it has done ever since. With Nos. 11 and 12 it is the only house in the street which has survived, if survived is the right word to use, in view of the fact that all three were pulled down and rebuilt in 1960–1963.

The Horse Guards.

10 Downing Street after rebuilding.

The Haymarket and Lincoln's Inn Fields

Ten minutes walk to the north of Downing St. was the Haymarket. A market for hay was still held there; but the principal attractions were two theatres.

At the Opera House, where Her Majesty's Theatre now stands, the operas of Handel were performed. (He had come to London in 1710.) At the New Theatre, which stood close to the site of the modern Haymarket Theatre, Fielding produced a number of his plays. Here, in 1736, Walpole took umbrage (pp. 9 and 199).

There were three other important London theatres—Drury Lane, and Lincoln's Inn Fields, both dating from the time of Charles II, and Covent Garden. In the second of these, which was managed by a Mr. Rich, *The Beggar's Opera* by John Gay was first produced on 29th January, 1728. Its tremendous success 'made Gay rich and Rich gay'. Here too John Rich began the performance of 'pantomimes' from which the traditional Christmas entertainment developed.

Lincoln's Inn Fields was an area in which the low-life characters of *The Beggar's Opera* would have felt at home. Though respectable people had lived there since the middle of the seventeenth century, they were slow to clean up the large rectangular area (bigger than the base of the Great Pyramid) which their houses overlooked. In 1729 the Fields had become:

> a receptacle for rubbish, dirt and nastiness of all sorts. Many wicked and disorderly persons have frequented and met together therein, using unlawful sports and games, and drawing in and enticing young persons into gaming, idleness and other vicious courses; and vagabonds, common beggars and other disorderly persons resort therein, where many robberies, assaults, outrages and enormities have been and continually are committed.

However, by the 1740's, when Tom Jones came to town, the residents had converted the Fields into a neat park with lawns and gravel paths and an iron fence round it. Anyway, with so many barristers close at hand in Lincoln's Inn* and Fielding's magistrate's court in Bow Street not very far away, a disorderly person could never have felt completely at ease. The Law Courts, however, were still in Westminster Hall and not yet on their present site to the south of Lincoln's Inn Fields.

Temple Bar was a solid stone gateway designed by Wren and now removed to the country. Heads or other parts of the bodies of men condemned as traitors were displayed upon it. In the years immediately after 1745 the heads were Highland, cut from the shoulders of chiefs who had fought for Bonnie Prince Charlie. For a halfpenny you could take a look at them through a telescope. This instrument had been invented by Galileo in the previous century.

Bloomsbury Church

A telescope would also have been useful for looking at the gilded statue of George I in Roman armour on the top of Bloomsbury Church (begun in 1716). The statue is still there, close to the east-bound bus stop for the British Museum. A rich brewer paid for it; Hawksmoor, surprisingly, designed it; Walpole called it 'a masterpiece of absurdity' and somebody wrote:

> When Henry the eighth left the Pope in the lurch,
> The Protestants made him the head of the Church;
> But George's good subjects, the Bloomsbury people,
> Instead of the Church, made him head of the steeple.

Wren and the City

Once you had passed through Wren's Temple Bar you could not forget him as long as you were within the City. Some fifty churches had been rebuilt to his

* See *The Elizabethan Age*.

Temple Bar with traitors' heads and a negro servant.

design after the Fire (1666) and St. Paul's towered above them. To reach it you crossed the Fleet by a bridge at what is now Ludgate Circus. Northwards the river had been covered in since 1737, but a smelly half mile of it still ran along a muddy channel above ground into the Thames.

St. Paul's, showing the balustrade (arrows). The tower on the left contains Great Tom. Cleaning had begun at that end and the tower was whiter than the rest of the Cathedral when the photograph was taken.

'Si monumentum requiris, circumspice' is the inscription on Wren's tomb in the crypt of St. Paul's—'If you want to find my monument, look around you.' Later tombs—Nelson's, for instance, and Wellington's, are more conspicuous; Wren's is not easy to find, so eager was he to emphasize the principle that the whole cathedral, and not just one stone in the crypt, was his monument.

Wren had prepared a scheme for the replanning of the whole City after the Fire (1666), but it was not accepted. The city was rebuilt; brick and stone houses replaced the wooden ones; but the area was not replanned. Narrow, ignoble streets remained.

Even St. Paul's was not finished as Wren had wished. The interior was never lined with gorgeous mosaics and outside the walls were topped with a balustrade, which Wren thought superfluous. 'Ladies think nothing well without an edging,' the old man complained. He was eighty-five and no doubt tiresome. Perhaps he was wrong about the balustrade. Look at it some day. But he was right in thinking that the City of London ought to have been replanned. Look at it too.

Modern lighting fitted into the 18th century ceiling of the Lord Mayor's Court room.

The Mansion House

The Bank of England was established in 1694 and by 1724 it already occupied part of the site in Threadneedle Street where its huge modern building now stands. Opposite is the Mansion House. Lord Mayors have expanded less than the Bank and still live in the home which was completed for them in 1752. (There had been no official residence before that. Dick Whittington* used his own house.) It has some very big rooms, e.g. a dining-room to seat about 400, and some very small ones, e.g. cells to accommodate prisoners who are dealt with in the Lord Mayor's Court.

* See *Chaucer's England*.

Nearby in Lombard Street was the General Post Office, whence letters were sent to all parts of Great Britain and abroad. The charge for a letter of one sheet sent up to 80 miles was 2d., more than 80 miles (inland) 3d. There was also a very convenient 1d. postal service within London. You could count on delivery in a few hours.

London Bridge and the watermen

Certain dilapidated relics of the Middle Ages which had escaped the Fire were still there in our period, e.g. London Bridge, crowded with houses, and parts of the old city walls with their massive gateways. Until Westminster Bridge was built in 1750, London Bridge carried the only road across the river.

Watermen still had plenty to do ferrying passengers for whom the crossing of the bridge was inconvenient. There were two kinds of boat. 'Sculls' were rowed by one man, 'oars' by two. The passenger shouted 'sculls' or 'next oars' when he reached the steps which led down to the river. In hot weather the waterman might fit a covering over hoops to protect his passengers. Fares were fixed and a printed list of them could be obtained, the charge for 'oars' being usually twice that for 'sculls'. Watermen, however, were not above asking for more. They had a rich vocabulary of insult which could be directed against passengers who kept to the standard rates.

'Barges' were available for pleasure trips. The word at that time meant a river boat with between 8 and 40 rowers and a good-sized cabin in the stern, fitted with a table and benches. Barges were used by the Lord Mayor and the City Companies, and by the Court. In a barge Handel performed his *Water Music* and from a barge the King listened to it.

There was a horse ferry between Westminster and

Lambeth (there is still a Horseferry Road). The fares were:

	s.	d.
Man and horse		2
Horse and chaise	1.	0
Coach and 2 horses	1.	6
,, ,, 4 ,,	2.	0
,, ,, 6 ,,	2.	6
Carts (loaded)	2.	6
,, (empty)	2.	0

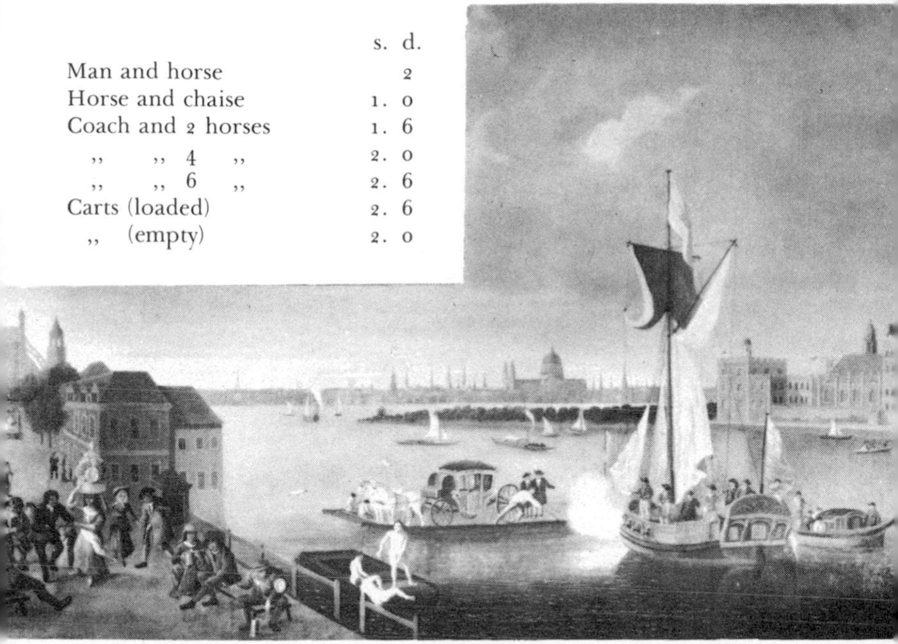

The horse ferry (above, *c.* 1700), near where Lambeth Bridge now crosses the Thames and a street (below) still bears the name. The old Houses of Parliament are on the left, St. Paul's in the background and Lambeth Palace on the right. The bathers are naked.

The transport by water of prisoners from their trial in Westminster Hall to the Traitors' Gate of the Tower of London was becoming less common. There were fewer traitors now. The last beheadings at the Tower were those of the Scottish chiefs after the 'forty-five'. But people still went to see the lions; the Tower had housed a little zoo since the time of Henry III; and the Mint was still there.

The coinage in the reigns of Anne and the first two Georges consisted of:

Gold	*Silver*	*Copper*
Five guineas	Crown	Halfpenny
Two guineas	Halfcrown	Farthing
Guinea	Shilling	
Half-guinea	Sixpence	
	Fourpence	
	Threepence	
	Twopence	
	Penny	

The copper coinage only came into regular use after Anne's death. Copper pennies were not minted until the end of the century.

Below London Bridge and east of the Tower Thames traffic grew thicker every year. The London Docks were not built till the nineteenth century. Before that every ship had to unload directly, or by means of lighters, at one of the quays along the riverside; and quayside space was limited. Britain's overseas trade was increasing and three-quarters of the goods imported came up the Thames. There was more and more coastal traffic too, in particular the boats laden with coal from Newcastle.

We have now crossed London from the fashionable west to the nautical east. Today's sprawling East End did not yet exist. The poorer, industrial quarters were

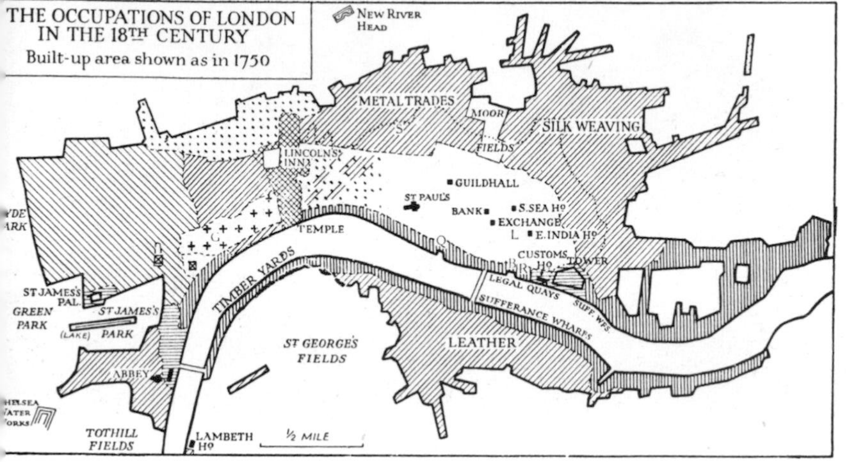

to the north, where the metal trades, especially clock-making and jewellery, were concentrated, and to the north-east where silk-weavers, many of them Huguenot refugees, occupied the Spitalfields area (now Shoreditch). Southwark was the home of tanning and kindred trades such as glue-making.

Food and water supply

The population of London during the first half of the eighteenth century was about three-quarters of a million. There was also a very large number of horses. The problems of supplying these men and animals with food and water were solved by private enterprise.

Food came by river or road to the great markets such as Smithfield, Covent Garden and Billingsgate. Often the man who grew the produce could bring it to market and sell it. But water supply needs capital. A number of companies had been formed. Most of them pumped water from the Thames. Pumps driven by water wheels had been installed under London Bridge in Elizabeth's time; they were destroyed in the Great Fire and rebuilt. They supplied water to the City and showed a good

Covent Garden (1737). Originally the Convent Garden of Westminster Abbey, it was built on in 1630—the first planned London square. Inigo Jones designed the Church. Now market buildings occupy most of the formerly open space. In the foreground a little girl puts money into the hat of a blind beggar with a dog. Behind, boxers fight, stripped to the waist, and a hackney coach drives by. On the left, vegetables are sold.

profit. In the waterworks which stood on the site of Charing Cross station and supplied Whitehall, Piccadilly and Covent Garden, one of Newcomen's steam engines was installed (1726). The 'New River', opened in 1613, brought water from Hertfordshire to a reservoir in Islington. But no water was purified and the main water pipes were of wood, though lead was used for connections to houses and to the public conduits on which most people still depended for their supply.

Sewage disposal

There was not much money to be made out of sewage disposal. Manure was collected from the streets and sold to farmers, but other cleaning operations required a municipal effort which even London was not yet prepared to make. Filth lay in the streets as it had done for centuries and the poorer, more crowded quarters stank. The Thames was the most obvious place for getting rid of sewage and there were sewers leading to it. But these sewers could only discharge easily at low water; the banks of the Thames were then loaded with filth, which contaminated the air; the rising tide carried the filth upstream and it returned on the ebb. Sometimes the Thames itself was like a gigantic sewer.

The problem of London sanitation was not seriously tackled until the authorities were terrified into activity by the cholera epidemics of the mid-nineteenth century. A Sewers Act had been passed in 1671. This created commissioners of sewers, who were responsible for the laying out and repair of streets as well as for keeping them clean and draining them. But the Act only applied to the City of London and the activities of the commissioners were of course limited by the money they had to spend. This was compulsorily contributed by householders.

Somehow, for one reason or another, the commissioners of sewers failed to fire the imagination of the public. The citizens had not been willing to build wide and noble streets after the Fire; they were equally unwilling to spend much on paving and draining such streets as were built. These were made of large round cobbles and there was no raised side-walk, though a line of posts gave some protection to pedestrians.

Cobbles, like potatoes, being laid at Hyde Park Corner in 1963, but only on an island where few people walk.

Hospitals

While failing to realize that neglect of cleanliness led to disease, many people were concerned about the lack of provision for invalids. To the existing hospitals—St. Bartholomew's and St. Thomas's—were added, by voluntary contributions, the Westminster (1720), Guy's (1724), St. George's (1733), The London (1740) and the Middlesex (1745).

But the mentally sick roused little sympathy. They were still confined in the Bethlehem Hospital, as they had been in medieval and Tudor times, and were still regarded as an entertaining spectacle. For twopence you could visit the wards and torment the patients. Only in 1750 was the more humane St. Luke's Hospital for Lunatics opened.

The Foundling Hospital (1739) provided a home for illegitimate children. It too was founded by voluntary effort. It should be remembered, particularly when the 'Trouble' chapter is read, that the early eighteenth century was not lacking in charity.

Street Lighting

In 1736 street lighting in the City was greatly improved. Before that year about a thousand lamps had been supplied and serviced by contractors, who collected six shillings a year from any householders who did not hang out a horn lantern with a candle in it at the front of their houses. But the contractors' lamps were only lit from the beginning of October to the end of March, they were put out at midnight and on ten so-called 'late nights' in every moon (i.e. from the sixth after the new moon to the third after the full) they were not lit at all, 'which short Space of lighting the Streets gave great Opportunities to Rogues to commit numerous

Captain Coram, founder of the Foundling Hospital with an abandoned baby. He still wears a sword as well as carrying a stick. This was unusual by the middle of the century.

Burglaries, Street Robberies, and other nocturnal Villainies'.

The City authorities now took the matter in hand. The alderman of each ward was made responsible for installing lamps, which were to be lit from sunset to sunrise throughout the year. Contributions by householders were increased and no one might contract out, except the Dean and Chapter of St. Paul's, who were allowed to light the fence round their cathedral.

How to get there

There was no public transport. Most people went about London on foot. Those who were very rich had private coaches, sometimes with as many as six horses—four driven by the coachman and the leading pair by a postilion, who rode one of them. For hire there were the Thames boats, hackney coaches drawn by two horses, and sedan chairs carried by two chairmen. 'Chairs', as they were called, had first become popular in Queen Anne's reign. Their charge, fixed by law, was a shilling a mile; a hackney coach had to go a mile and a half for the same fare. Chairs were convenient for short distances in crowded streets—convenient, that is to say, for the occupants; they could be a nuisance to pedestrians. The poet Gay complained:

> When e'er I pass, their Poles, unseen below,
> Make my knee tremble with the jarring blow.

Not that the passenger was free from jarring. He or she often had a rough ride, followed by a wrangle about the fare. When Squire Western came to London in pursuit of his daughter, Sophia, he gave a tip of 6d. in addition to the legal shilling fare. The chairmen took this as a sign, not of generosity, but of a countryman's ignorance; so they demanded another shilling, which they did not get. 'Damn me, if I won't walk in the rain rather than get into one of their hand-barrows again,' said the Squire afterwards. 'They have jolted me more in a mile than Brown Bess would in a long fox-chase.'

Chairmen were tough. If you were well dressed and did not hire them they abused you; if they had to wait a long time outside a house they passed the time making ribald comments about what you might be doing inside.

The only form of transport which took a number of passengers at the same time was the stage coach. It carried six passengers inside and several on top, at a cost to each of about threepence a mile. But the coaches did not ply for hire in town. You only took one if you wanted to leave London; which we must now do, like *The Beggar's Opera,* of which a newspaper wrote, only three months after the show had opened in London, that it 'has already strollen into the Country; it has been seen at Dover to great advantage, and it is expected at Norwich, and, it's thought, will make a general Progress thro the Kingdom this summer'.

Gentleman removed from a sedan and arrested for debt by the Sheriff's officers. The rear chairman lifts the roof to allow the chair to open. The lamp man watches the scene instead of the lamp which he is refilling. (Hogarth).

'Town bias'

You may have noticed that 'Country' in the above quotation in fact means a series of towns. To a travelling theatrical company the countryside is simply the bits of England between the towns. Towns get more than their share of prominence on maps too. On a map of England—even an eighteenth century map—what strikes the eye is a network of roads joining hundreds of named towns. One has to remind oneself that the nameless gaps in between are the country and that in our period its inhabitants were more numerous than those in the towns.

This book is 'town-biased'. In particular it is London-biased. There is always more happening in a town and its history is more fully recorded. This is especially true of London. It was true even in a period like the first half of the eighteenth century, before England was industrialized. Fielding hoped to interest his readers more by bringing Tom Jones and Parson Adams to London. Moll Flanders lived there and from time to time when she left London, it was always to go to another town—Bath, for example, or Dunstable or Colchester.

Growth of towns

In 1700, as in Elizabethan times, the two biggest towns after London were Bristol and Norwich, centres of the wool trade, which was still England's chief industry. York, the second city of England in medieval times, had fallen far behind in size and importance (though it has a number of eighteenth century buildings still). In the years which followed it was the turn of Bristol and Norwich to lose their high positions. By the end of the century the order (by size of population)

was: London, Manchester, Liverpool, Birmingham, Bristol, Leeds, Plymouth, Norwich. These changes were already taking place during our period, although towns grew more rapidly during the second half of the eighteenth century.

It is not possible in the space of this book to describe more than a few towns. Readers who live in other English towns, all with interesting histories, must search out for themselves the answer to the question: 'What was —ingham or —bury like in the eighteenth century?'

Bristol

Like many of the older towns at this time, Bristol still had its medieval walls. Such fortifications were of little use in England after the Civil War, but Bristolians had retired behind theirs during Monmouth's rebellion (1685). The streets were narrow and dirty. Dog-drawn sledges were used for carrying goods. Water could be drawn from a number of public conduits. But above the mean streets rose, in 1743, the Corn Exchange. This can still be seen. So can Wesley's first Methodist chapel (1739).

Bristol was not only the second city, but also the second port of England after London. Avonmouth Docks had not yet been built. Sea-going ships came up the river into the city, as some smaller ones still do. Bristol is built at the junction of two rivers, the Avon and the Frome. This was a great advantage, since it provided extra mooring space for ships and helped to solve the city's sewage problems.

What were the cargoes? Outward bound ships took cloth and metal goods (the amount of the latter increased as the wool trade moved north). Of the inward bound ships some had only crossed from South Wales with coal or from Ireland with wool, flax or cattle.

Others had brought copper round the coast from Cornwall, or wines and salt from France, Spain or Portugal. Larger vessels unloaded tobacco from Virginia, or sugar and rum from the West Indies; but these tasty trans-Atlantic cargoes had been bought at a shameful price, with shiploads of slaves. The Treaty of Utrecht (1714) had given England almost a monopoly of the slave trade. Nearly two-thirds of the ships that sailed from Bristol were slavers.

Bristolians did not see the slaves, who were taken direct from West Africa across the Atlantic. But Bristolians saw the money. A good place in which to spend it was Bath.

Bath

'Bath is a place of gallantry enough; expensive, and full of snares.' This is the comment of Defoe's Moll Flanders. Richard Nash, who became known as 'Beau Nash', was 'master of the ceremonies' at Bath in 1705 and made it the most fashionable holiday resort in England. Many people went simply for the social life—concerts, dancing, gambling and talking; but some also bathed in or drank the medicinal waters.

Near Bath Fielding wrote part of *Tom Jones,* the earlier

Sham Castle, a sham medieval building, put up by Ralph Allen at Bath to improve the view from his town house.

chapters of which are set in Somersetshire. The characters wander about Gloucestershire before finding their way to London, not along the Bath road, but by way of Gloucester, Coventry and St. Albans.

Large cheese biscuits called Bath Olivers were first made in Bath in 1735. The manufacture continued there till 1963, when it was moved to Reading.

It was a Bath postmaster, Ralph Allen, who in 1721 was permitted to organize a service of 'cross-posts' direct between provincial towns. Previously all letters had passed through London. Allen increased the revenues of the Post Office by his system and made a fortune. He was a great benefactor of the City of Bath and Squire Allworthy in *Tom Jones* is thought to be a portrait of him.

Birmingham

Birmingham had been famous for its metal industries since the time of Henry VIII. Birmingham smiths had made thousands of sword blades for the Parliamentary forces during the Civil War. (They refused to supply the Royalists.) By the beginning of the eighteenth century other industries were growing, e.g. the manufacture of guns and brassware, and the town was growing. In 1711 a new church, St. Philip's, was built. (It is now the cathedral.)

At this time, with about 15,000 inhabitants, Birmingham was among the 20 biggest towns in the kingdom. By the end of the century, with 74,000, it was fourth.

William Hutton, arriving in 1741 and having previously only known smaller places like Nottingham, Derby and Lichfield, was thrilled by Birmingham. 'I was surprised at the place, but more at the people. They possessed a vivacity I had never beheld... Every man seemed to know what he was about.'

Why was this? One reason may have been that

Ralph Allen's cross-post system.

Birmingham was not 'corporate', i.e. an ancient city or borough. Bristol was, and Defoe thought that what he called 'the tenacious folly of its inhabitants' sprang from this. They were cursed with 'the general infatuation, the pretence of freedoms and privileges, that corporation-tyranny, which prevents the flourishing and increase of many a good town in England'. In short, they kept out new men. Not so Birmingham. There was the further point that the Five Mile Act (1665) forbade nonconformist ministers to live in a corporate town; but nothing prevented them from living in Birmingham. It became a centre where nonconformists and Jews were happy to settle. They did the town much good.

Manchester

Manchester was not a borough and sent no member to Parliament, but it was a growing town (about 10,000 in 1717), where the textile industry was already well established. A body called the Court Leet dealt with the usual town problems, such as sewerage and water supplies, control of markets and punishment of crimes not serious enough to await the Quarter Sessions or the Assizes at Lancaster. The town contained some elegant buildings; St. Ann's church was opened in 1712; but near it cattle grazed and pigs ran about the unpaved streets. There were green meadows and a pond where Piccadilly now runs and sailing boats could be seen on the Irwell.

After being Puritan in sympathy during the previous century Manchester now favoured the Jacobites. The town was occupied by the Young Pretender in 1745 and raised a regiment to support him. By 1801, with 84,000 inhabitants, Manchester-Salford was second in size to London.

On one of the journeys which Moll Flanders made to different parts of England in the hope of finding a rich husband or of somehow improving her fortunes, she travelled with a female friend to Lancashire. '. . . and her brother brought a gentleman's coach to Warrington to receive us; and we were carried from there to Liverpool with as much ceremony as I could desire. We were also entertained at a merchant's house in Liverpool three or four days very handsomely.'

Where did the merchant's money come from? Though a borough, Liverpool had not been important before the Restoration. A population of not much more than 1,000 had traded with Ireland, France and Spain. After the Restoration the rise of industry in Lancashire and the opening up of trade with the West Indies and America sent Liverpool's population figure from 6,000 to 78,000 in the course of the eighteenth century, by the end of which it was the third city in the United Kingdom. So some Liverpudlians made a great deal of money. Towards the beginning of the eighteenth century they built the first wet dock in England, began, like Bristol, to engage in the slave trade and acquired a high degree of skill in defrauding the customs officers of the duty payable on tobacco.

Meanwhile the Town Council had to deal with the usual municipal problems. They provided street lamps (but citizens had to keep them filled with oil at their own expense). They kept two fire-engines in readiness. They insisted on the construction of a 'convenient Hole with an Iron Gate over it at every Street End' for muck; the holes were to be cleared on Mondays and Thursdays. And so that the Mayor could keep himself up to date, he was authorized to buy a London newspaper—the *St. James's Evening Post*—at the Corporation's expense.

The stage coach (Hogarth, 1747). Seats were not yet provided on the roof, but there were usually handles to hold. The old lady in the luggage basket smokes contentedly, but when the coach goes fast downhill, bundles and parcels will bounce against her. On the wall above is the inn sign—*The Old Angel* and the name of the proprietor, Tom Bates. Bates himself (fat, left of coach steps) presents a bill to a suspicious-looking guest, while another guest kisses the chambermaid in the doorway. The scene shows the courtyard of the inn, with its wooden gallery.

Newcastle upon Tyne

Although the coal trade, ship-building and the production of iron and steel were all expanding in the neighbourhood, Newcastle itself still looked like a medieval town, when George III came to the throne. Its wall with seven gates protected the 20,000 citizens so effectively in 1715 and 1745 that both the Old and the Young Pretender decided to leave them alone and enter England by Carlisle.

One bridge, lined with houses and shops, spanned

the river. It had changed little since Chaucer's time. Streets were unlit, except where householders hung a lantern by their doors, and there was no public drainage system. But a public hospital with ninety beds, paid for by subscriptions, was built in 1752, and in 1755 a bank was opened, one of the first in the country outside London.

John Wesley found the poor of Newcastle very receptive to his preaching. To him 'no place in Britain was comparable to it in pleasantness'.

Roads

What were the roads like? The answer to this question in every period of English history between the departure of the Romans and the end of the eighteenth century is that the roads were bad. Towards the end of the seventeenth century Parliament sanctioned the first 'Turnpike Trusts'. These were groups of men who took over the maintenance of a stretch of road and were then allowed to charge fees for its use. (This system of paying a toll for the use of an improved road is now used on some continental motorways.)

The coachman.

When the Turnpike Trusts first set to work in England, the system had the weakness that not enough of the money collected by the gatekeeper and paid to the trustees was in fact used to improve the road. Here and there useful work was done, particularly near London, where trustees used the roads themselves. But the turnpike system did not make an appreciable difference to travel during the first half of the eighteenth century. Most roads were still grudgingly and indifferently maintained by the parish through which they passed and, of those which had been turnpiked, not all had been improved.

Manchester is 184 miles from London and in 1754 an advertisement for a Flying Coach stated that:

> However incredible it may appear, this coach will actually (barring accidents) arrive in London in 4 days and a half.

On a fine summer day a good coach-and-four took from 5 a.m. to 8 p.m. to travel from London to Cambridge (53 miles). Trevelyan *(England under Queen Anne)* points out that undergraduates have walked the journey more quickly in modern times.

For goods, pack mules or river transport were much used (canals were developed later in the century). Most travellers, like Tom Jones on his way to London, walked or rode on horseback. A bad road surface was less of an obstacle to them than it was to a coach. Tom Jones and his companion once wandered off the Coventry road by mistake, but only because it was dark and raining. As soon as Jones came by some money, he 'travelled post', changing horses regularly, and his progress towards London was quick. There were posthouses at regular intervals all over the kingdom. Horses had to be provided not only for the 'postboys' (they were sometimes retired cavalrymen) carrying the mails but also for all travellers prepared to pay the charge of 3d. a mile.

Road surfaces do not seem to have infuriated Fielding nearly as much as the people who travelled over them or made a living out of travellers—lazy postboys, insolent innkeepers, cantankerous coachmen. When Joseph Andrews had been stripped by robbers and left naked in a ditch by the roadside, a stage coach drew up. Joseph's groans were heard by the postilion and the coachman was persuaded to stop. The following were among the comments then made:

Coachman: 'Go on, sirrah, we are confounded late, and have no time to look after dead men.'

A lady passenger: 'O Jesus, a naked man! Dear coachman, drive on and leave him.'

An old gentleman passenger: 'Robbed! Let us make all the haste imaginable, or we shall be robbed too.'

People

On the whole Fielding's characters are either very sour or very sweet. That was how he liked them. He had plenty to choose from. The population of England

'The poor, that fare hard'.

'The rich, who live very plentifully' (Edith Evans as Miss Western, David Warner as Blifil). Look again at this when reading the section on Clothes in Chapter 2.

and Wales has been estimated at about five and a half million in 1700. By 1760 it had risen to about seven million. Today the population is forty-five million. Advertisers have to estimate the proportion of the population which belongs to each class. A five-class scale is widely used. Here it is, with percentages for a recent year:

A	4%	The well-to-do
B	8%	The middle class
C	17%	The lower middle class
D	64%	The working class
E	7%	The poor, including old age pensioners.

Writing in 1707 Defoe suggested that the people of England could be divided into seven classes (he had of course no means of estimating the numbers in each). Here they are:

1. The great, who live profusely
2. The rich, who live very plentifully
3. The middle sort, who live well
4. The working trades, who labour hard but feel no want
5. The country people, farmers, etc., who fare indifferently
6. The poor, that fare hard
7. The miserable, that really pinch and suffer want

CHAPTER II

AT HOME

WHAT IS a palace? Apart from the royal palaces in London and Edinburgh and the residences of archbishops and bishops, how many lived-in palaces are there in Britain?

There is a useful periodical published every year, which lists hundreds of homes and gardens open to the public. In it you can find Castles, Halls, Manors, Parks, Towers, Abbeys, Houses and Courts, but only one Palace—Blenheim

Blenheim Palace

Blenheim was a big, prompt prize to the Duke of Marlborough for his great victory over the French at Blenheim, on the Danube, in August 1704. I call it 'prompt' because, although building went on for many years, the foundation stone was laid only ten months after the victory.

It was on August 13th, 1704, that Marlborough, still on horseback, used the back of a tavern bill supplied by one of his officers, to send news to his wife, Sarah. Smoothing out the bill on his saddle he wrote, in pencil:

> I have not time to say more, but to beg you will give my duty to the Queen, and let her know Her Army has had a glorious victory . . .

Blenheim in 1745. Skirts are wide and few men wear swords.

An officer took eight days to deliver this letter in London, and a thanksgiving service was held in the unfinished cathedral of St. Paul's on September 7th. During the autumn and winter Queen Anne considered how best to reward Marlborough and 'perpetuate the memory of his great services'. She had already made him a Duke; so she now decided to present him with an estate. In February 1705 she told the House of Commons that she had chosen Woodstock near Oxford. Woodstock had been a royal estate for centuries. Elizabeth I had lived there for a time before she was Queen. But the house was now a ruin. Anne directed that a splendid palace should be built, at the royal expense.

Sir John Vanbrugh

Who was to be the architect? Sir Christopher Wren, Surveyor of the Board of Works, was the obvious man and he did in fact travel to Woodstock to prepare an estimate of the cost of the palace. But Sir John Vanbrugh was chosen to design the building. No one knows for certain why he was preferred. At this time he was better known as a playwright than as an architect. On the other hand he was in his forties, while Wren was over seventy, and Vanbrugh's design for Castle Howard, which was then being built in Yorkshire, may have impressed the Duke of Marlborough.

Vanbrugh lost no time and on June 19th, 1705 a Woodstock paper reported as follows:

> Yesterday being Monday, about six o'clock in the evening, was laid the first stone of the Duke of Marlborough's House, by Mr. Vanbrugge [i.e. Vanbrugh], and then seven gentlemen gave it a stroke with a hammer, and threw down each of them a guinea. Sir Thomas Wheate was the first, Dr. Bouchel the second, Mr. Vanbrugge the third; I know not the rest. There were several sorts of musick; three morris dances; one of young fellows, one of maidens, and one of old beldames. There were about a hundred buckets, bowls and pans, filled with wine, punch, cakes and ale. From my lord's house all went to the Town-hall, where plenty of sack, claret, cakes, etc., were prepared for the gentry and better sort; and under the Cross eight barrels of ale, with abundance of cakes, were placed for the common people.

By August, fifteen hundred workmen were on the site and several quarries had been opened in the park; but these only supplied stone fit for inside walls; better stone had to be carted from two quarries, one three, and the other five miles away. When these were exhausted, many others much more distant had to be used. Hundreds of carters had to be employed. In winter the weather delayed them and in summer they were needed for the harvest. Masons too had to be brought from afar, not only from London, but from 'the Remotest Countys in the Kingdom'. This increased the wage bill. But Vanbrugh had a competent young clerk of the works under him, and the building of the house went on.

A number of artists and craftsmen who had been working on St. Paul's now moved to Blenheim. Of them the most famous is Grinling Gibbons, who had carved wooden choir stalls in many city churches and now had to work on huge pieces of stone sculpture which ornamented the outside of the palace.

The gardens

In laying out the park and gardens, Vanbrugh had the help of Henry Wise, the Queen's gardener. The design was formal. Geometrical patterns were used. English gardeners had long followed this continental practice. Soon there was to be a great change. 'Landscape gardening' was introduced and the great landscape gardener, 'Capability Brown' (p. 59), took Blenheim in hand. But in 1705 Marlborough knew nothing of such things. While he fought in Flanders he kept in touch with Vanbrugh and left him in no doubt that he dreamed of a garden full of fruit and flowers. This Mr. Wise provided. Here are some items from the bills which had to be paid, beginning with young fruit trees. The spelling has not been brought up to date:

29	Apricocks	at	1s	each
134	Plums	at	9d	each
262	Aples and Codlings	at	8d	each
400	Goosberries and currants	at	1½d	each
190	Vines	at	6d	each
32	ffiggs	at	2s	each
500	Sweet Bryers	at	1d	each
5,100	Hyacinths	at	6s	a hundred
18,500	Dutch Yellow Crocus	at	1s 6d	a hundred
4,600	Tulips	at	10s	a hundred

Among the flowers were many varieties of Brompton Stock, carnations, violets, marigolds and damask roses, while the kitchen garden was to include four kinds of lettuce, peas, beans, cabbage, 'colliflower', turnips, parsnips, leeks, onions, black Spanish 'reddish', cress and 'sallery' (celery). Celery had just been introduced from France by Marshall Tallard, who was living comfortably at Nottingham after his capture by Marlborough at the battle of Blenheim.

In the summer of 1707, when the fruit trees had had time to establish themselves, Marlborough wrote to his wife:

> I would wish that you might, or somebody else you can rely on, taste the fruit of every tree, so that what is not good might be changed. On this matter you must advise with Mr. Wise, as also what plan may be proper for the ice-house; for that should be built this summer, so that it might have time to dry. The hot weather makes me think of these things . . .

The only way of having ice in summer was to collect it in winter, e.g. from the lake when it froze, and store it in an ice-house.

Who pays?

During the winter, when eighteenth century armies did not fight, the Duke was able to return to England and see how the building of the palace was progressing. He found that the Treasury had not been sending money regularly, so the carriers had not been paid and had therefore ceased to carry. There was a shortage of stone. An appeal had been sent to the Treasury: 'Grant money Speedyly or wee ffeare a ffull stopp in our Business'. A quite inadequate sum had been sent. Payments to everyone on the job were constantly in arrears, but somehow, except during very bad weather, building went on.

The Duchess of Marlborough had thought Blenheim an extravagant undertaking from the first, or so she wrote later. Now she began to quarrel with Vanbrugh over items of expenditure. He for instance wanted to preserve what remained of Woodstock Manor, the former royal residence. The Duchess said it should be pulled down and eventually it was. But the quarrel over

Vanbrugh's bridge over the lake at Blenheim.

it lasted for years and relations between Vanbrugh and the Duchess grew worse.

Another disagreement was over the Grand Bridge which was to cross the ornamental lake. The Duchess thought Vanbrugh had made it much too big and complained that she had counted thirty-three rooms in it. Anyone who goes to Blenheim should inspect the bridge at close quarters. It is certainly comparable in capacity to a good-sized house, but the interior is unsafe, so members of the public cannot now check the Duchess's count of the rooms. Vanbrugh got his own way over the bridge. The rooms later provided a 'cool retreat in summer' for residents at Blenheim, and one of the arches housed a water-driven engine which pumped water from a nearby spring along oak pipes to a cistern over the east gate of the palace. (You can still see the cistern and part of the engine is in Old Woodstock Mill.)

During the last years of Anne's reign (1712-1714),

both the Duke and Duchess were out of favour and lived abroad, the Treasury stopped paying for Blenheim altogether, and work came to a standstill.

When Anne died in 1714, the Marlboroughs returned but, although they were welcomed by George I, he was not prepared to go on bearing the cost of Blenheim. The Treasury made a payment which only settled about a third of the outstanding debts, and when work on the palace began again (1716), the Marlboroughs had to pay for it themselves. In this same year the Duchess's quarrel with Vanbrugh came to a head and he resigned. Not until 1720 was the east wing of Blenheim far enough advanced for the Duchess to consent to move in. The palace was completed in 1722 and in that year the Duke died; so he had little enjoyment from the nation's gift (his family motto was 'faithful but unfortunate'). We should thank him for Blenheim, rather than he us.

Vanbrugh's death

Vanbrugh died in 1726. He never had more than a distant view of Blenheim after its completion, but he

Castle Howard.

built other great houses (Castle Howard in Yorkshire, Seaton Delaval near Newcastle and Kimbolton Castle, Huntingdonshire, can be visited today). Late in life he married. Lady Mary Wortley Montagu, perhaps remembering the famous quarrel over old Woodstock Manor, spitefully commented in a letter:

> Van's taste was always odd, his inclination to ruins has given him a fancy for Miss Yarburgh.

Spiteful too was the epitaph suggested for Vanbrugh:

> Lie heavy, earth, on him, for he
> Laid many a heavy load on thee.

The lines might have amused him. He was not hypersensitive. 'I am not one of those', he once wrote, 'who

Entrance hall of Clandon Park.

drop their Spirits on every Rebuff: if I had, I had been under ground long ago.'

Other houses to see

Other great country houses built or remodelled during the first half of the eighteenth century and all now at times open to visitors are, with their architects:

Holkham Hall, Norfolk (William Kent)
Wolterton Hall, Norfolk (Thomas Ripley)
Clandon Park, Surrey (Leoni)
Mereworth Castle, Kent (Colen Campbell)
Stoneleigh Abbey, Kenilworth, Warwickshire (Francis Smith)
Stourhead Zeals, Wiltshire (Colen Campbell)
Badminton House, Gloucester (William Kent)
Woburn Abbey, Bedfordshire (Flitcroft)
Lyme Park, Cheshire (Leoni)
Ebberston Hall, Yorkshire (Colen Campbell)

The Palladian style

What have these houses in common? Most of them are built of stone and in what is called the 'Palladian' style. Palladio was an Italian architect of the sixteenth century who introduced a simple classical style of building. This style was followed by Inigo Jones in early seventeenth century England and was still popular when building started again after the Civil War.

In the latter part of the seventeenth century sash windows were introduced from Holland. Corridors were a new development at the beginning of the eighteenth century (hitherto rooms had opened out of one another). At this period too the staircase began to be kept out of the entrance hall, which thus became simply a vast and impressive area for the reception and seeing-off of guests. Outside the front door was a wide flight of stone steps, made necessary by the fact that the hall and main rooms were no longer built at ground level but had a basement below them.

Staircase at Kensington Palace, decorated by William Kent. Arches, pillars and people are all painted on a flat wall. Notice the candle-holder on the right.

William Kent

Among the names of architects listed on p. 57, the most famous is William Kent. He had studied painting in Italy and on returning to England worked as a painter, sculptor, designer of furniture and architect; but his greatest success was in landscape gardening. He was one of those who put into practice the suggestions of literary men like Steele and Pope, who wanted parks and gardens to look less artificial and more as if they had been formed by nature.

In order that people looking out of the windows of their country houses should have an uninterrupted view of fields, woods or far-off hills, Kent introduced sunken walls and fences which could not be seen from a distance. They were called 'ha-ha's'—'ha-ha' being the expression of merriment, surprise and delight with which some visitors greeted these ingenious new devices.

Art however was not excluded from these 'natural' landscape gardens. At Stowe in Buckinghamshire, where Kent redesigned the park for Sir Richard Temple (afterwards Lord Cobham), he included thirty-eight temples. A visitor who thought this too many said: 'Sir Richard has been led astray by his name.' Bridges and artificial ruins were another form of decoration with which Kent liked to improve the views which he created for his clients.

Stowe is now a boarding school, but there are days in the year when the grounds are open.

Capability Brown

Though an enthusiast for nature, Kent did not wield the spade himself nor indulge in other healthy exercise. 'High feeding and an inactive life' brought on an illness from which he died in 1748. Meanwhile, in 1740, a young man named Lancelot Brown had started work in the kitchen garden at Stowe. Brown did not stay in the kitchen garden. He was a practical man—a northerner of poor parents, who had come south to better himself. He became head gardener at Stowe, helped to carry out the alterations planned by Kent and was soon designing landscape gardens himself. After looking over an estate whose owner had consulted him, he would say 'Yes, the place has capabilities of improvement, great capabilities.' He thus became known as 'Capability Brown'. But most of his greater work, which included the redesigning of the park at Blenheim (1764-1774), was done after the period covered by this book.

Redecorating Marlborough House, which is now used for Commonwealth conferences.

Town Houses

As Blenheim is the most famous country house built during the first half of the eighteenth century, so Marlborough House is the most famous of those built in town. Undeterred by the burden of Vanbrugh's colossal project at Woodstock (begun in 1705), the Duchess of Marlborough in 1708 acquired a site beside St. James's Palace. At this time Marlborough was at the height of his fame and his Duchess was still Queen Anne's closest friend. Wren, now in his seventy-sixth year, was to be the architect. He did not have to worry about the quarrying and transport of stone. Like most

Dr. Johnson's House, near Fleet St. It is
en to the public. For the other side of the
or, see p. 209.

town houses, Marlborough House was built of brick. As the Duke was campaigning in the Netherlands, he was able to arrange for bricks to be bought there, where they were cheaper, and brought over to England as ballast on army transport ships. The house was finished in 1711. It has been much altered and enlarged since then and is open to the public at certain times, when not in use for government conferences.

North of St. James's Palace and Marlborough House, as noted in Chapter I, were the great squares. In 1708 a fashionable lady was house-hunting for her son, who was abroad. She found a house which she liked at the corner of St. James's Square and what is now Charles II Street and described it in letters to her son. Below are extracts, in the original spelling. 'Wenscoat' = 'Wainscot' which means wood panelling. Plaster walls became more usual in the first half of the eighteenth century. 'Offisses' = 'offices', a term still used by estate agents to describe kitchen quarters and outbuildings. Note that there is no mention of bathrooms or water closets, not because the writer is bashful but because these amenities were almost unknown at the time. The 'closetts' mentioned are cupboards.

My dearist and best of children, I have been to see a very good hous in St. Jamsis Squair. It has thre large rooms forward and two little ons backward, closetts and marble chimney-peicis, and harths to al the best rooms and iron backs to the chimneys. Thear is picturs in the wenscoat over most of the chimneys, bras locks to all the doars, wenscoat at bottom and top and slips of boards for the hangings. Thear will want little to be dun to it. Thear is back stairs twoe coach housis, and stable for 11 horsis, rooms over for sarvents, very good offisses, a yard for the drying of cloaths and leds for that purpas, a stable-yard and a hors pond, and back gate, which I forget the street's name it goes into. Thear is a handsom roome al wenscoated for the steward to dyne in, and another good roome for the other sarvents to dyne in even with the kitchin belowestairs under the hall and parlors. It was my Lord Sunderland's, it was to little for them. To-morrow the man comes to tell me the prise. Indeed it is a noble hous, you may build a gallary over the offesis; they say this hous is soe strong it will last for ever . . . He the caretaker asurse me none of the chimneys smoke, and thear is New Rever water in all the offesis and great led sesterns in twoe or thre playsis, the kitchin is one and the brew-hous and wash-hous. Thear is a large chimney and grate and five stoavs in the kitchin. He ses the locks are worth £30, then thear is picturs over the chimney . . . Dear soul, my paper is al fild with thees housis, I wish the best of them were fild with you and all your goods, with the adetion of a good, buitefull, vertious wife, to the great comfort of, my dearist dear, your most infenite affectionat Mother.

Hogarth's House, Chiswick. His mulberry tree is on the left. The house was built in Queen Anne's reign, and is open to the public.

Room of about 1730 taken from a house in Hatton Garden, City of London, and reconstructed in the Victoria and Albert Museum. It is panelled in pinewood and originally would have been painted olive green, blue, brown, buff or white. Carving was sometimes partly gilded.

Inside the house

The house described in the above letter no longer exists, but, in addition to the great houses listed on p. 57, plenty of smaller ones survive from the first half of the eighteenth century. They often contain furniture and fittings of the period. Some museums have a reconstructed eighteenth century room. There is one, at the Victoria and Albert Museum in London. It is the kind of dining-room in which Tom Jones might have been entertained in London.

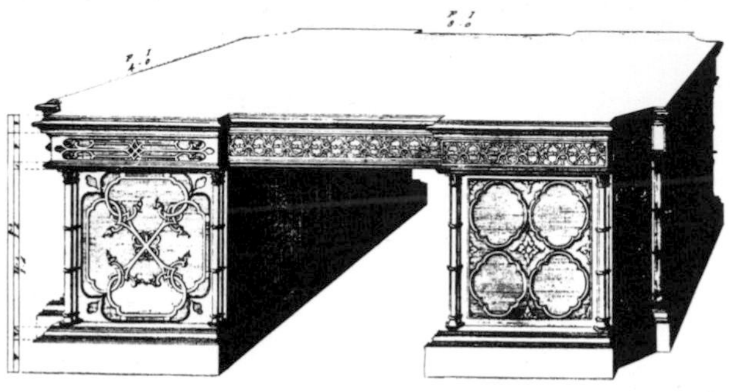

The golden age of English furniture

The year 1754, when Fielding died, was also the year in which *The Gentleman and Cabinet-Maker's Director,* by Thomas Chippendale, was published. In 1758 Robert Adam returned from a period of study in Italy and soon became the foremost architect and designer in the United Kingdom. The years which followed produced furniture and interior decoration of rare quality which still commands enormous prices. (Decoration does not necessarily disappear with a house. An Adam fireplace, for instance, can be saved and sold. I saw one recently in a new house in Belgium.) Most of this falls outside our period. But already in the first half of the eighteenth century furniture was better made and much more varied than in Elizabethan times.

THE

GENTLEMAN

AND

CABINET-MAKER's

DIRECTOR.

BEING A LARGE

COLLECTION

OF THE MOST

Elegant and Uſeful Deſigns of Houſhold Furniture

IN THE

GOTHIC, CHINESE and MODERN TASTE:

Including a great VARIETY of

BOOK-CASES for LIBRARIES or Private ROOMS. COMMODES,
LIBRARY and WRITING-TABLES,
BUROES, BREAKFAST-TABLES,
DRESSING and CHINA-TABLES,
CHINA-CASES, HANGING-SHELVES,
TEA-CHESTS, TRAYS, FIRE-SCREENS,
CHAIRS, SETTEES, SOPHA'S, BEDS,
PRESSES and CLOATHS-CHESTS,
PIER-GLASS SCONCES, SLAB FRAMES,
BRACKETS, CANDLE-STANDS,
CLOCK-CASES, FRETS,

AND OTHER

ORNAMENTS.

TO WHICH IS PREFIXED,

A Short EXPLANATION of the Five ORDERS of ARCHITECTURE, and RULES of PERSPECTIVE;

WITH

Proper DIRECTIONS for executing the moſt difficult Pieces, the Mouldings being exhibited at large, and the Dimenſions of each DESIGN ſpecified:

THE WHOLE COMPREHENDED IN

One Hundred and Sixty COPPER-PLATES, neatly Engraved,

Calculated to improve and refine the preſent TASTE, and ſuited to the Fancy and Circumſtances of Perſons in all Degrees of Life.

Dulcique animos novitate tenebo. OVID.
Ludentis ſpeciem dabit & torquebitur. HOR.

BY

THOMAS CHIPPENDALE,

Of St. *MARTIN*'s-*LANE*, CABINET-MAKER. K

LONDON,

Printed for the AUTHOR, and ſold at his Houſe in St. MARTIN's-LANE. MDCCLIV.
Alſo by T. OSBORNE, Bookſeller, in Gray's-Inn; H. PIERS, Bookſeller, in Holborn; R. SAYER, Print-ſeller, in Fleetſtreet; J. SWAN, near Northumberland-Houſe, in the Strand. At EDINBURGH, by Meſſrs. HAMILTON and BALFOUR: And at DUBLIN, by Mr. JOHN SMITH, on the Blind-Quay.

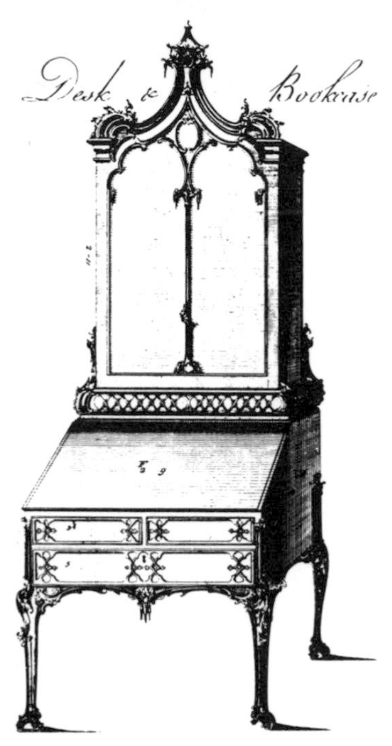

Furniture in Fielding's time

Beds still had four posts with heavy curtains and candles were still the most usual form of artificial light; but oak storage chests were being replaced by chests of drawers, often made of walnut, and towards the middle of the century, washstands began to appear. In the downstairs rooms furniture had changed, because habits had changed. Tea-drinking and card-playing needed small tables. Books needed bookcases. Ornamental china, the collection of which was now fashionable, had to be kept in a glass-fronted cabinet. Knowing the right time had also become important, simply because it was now possible. The making of accurate and beautiful watches and clocks had become a great English industry after the Restoration. Every well furnished house contained one of the new grandfather clocks.

Silver candlestick (1754), one of a set of four sold for £500 in 1963.

Wine glass of about 1735, when Houghton Hall was built. Engraved on it are the words 'Prosperity to Houghton'.

Laying the table

A dinner table in the house of a man of means was a fine sight. On a shining white tablecloth fine silverware sparkled. Knife-blades were duller, because they were not yet made of stainless steel, but their handles might be of silver or porcelain. Beside each was a matching fork, probably with only two prongs, though three-pronged ones were beginning to appear. The two prongs were very sharp. They would hold a piece of meat while you cut it, but great care was

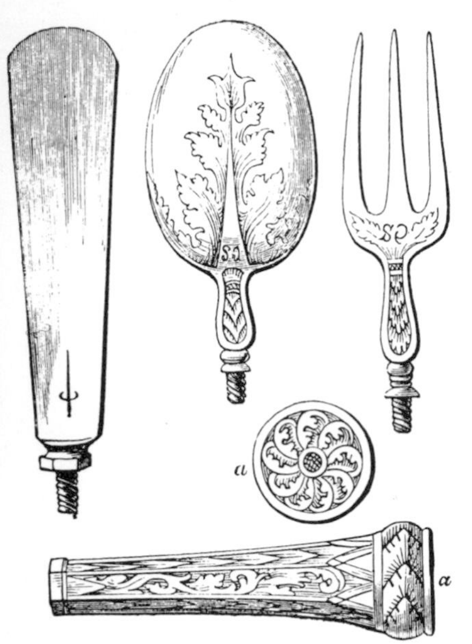

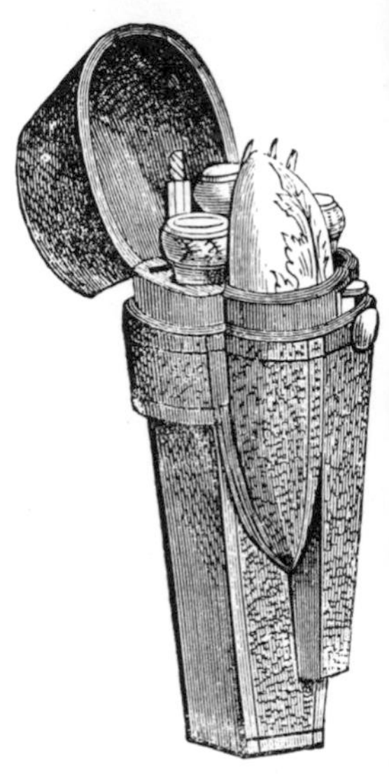

(*Left*) Pocket knife, fork and spoon of Charles Edward Stuart ('Bonnie Prince Charlie'). Only one of the three screw-on handles is shown. The pattern on its end is shown at 'a'. (*Right*) The cutlery packed for travelling.

necessary if they were used for conveying food to the mouth. A silver spoon might also be provided. When the food was finished the cloth was removed. The candles in their silver sticks were then reflected in the polished table-top, and brilliant, slender English wine glasses contrasted with the squat dark wine bottle as it was passed around.

Carpets and Wallpapers

Carpets were imported in large numbers from the east and workshops for making them were opened in England (e.g. at Axminster). A well furnished house now had carpeted floors.

Decorated paper had been known since the sixteenth century, but had been used more for lining boxes and chests than for walls. It was during our period that plaster walls covered with paper began to replace panelling or 'wainscot'. Sometimes the paper was already decorated with a pattern when it was hung. Sometimes white paper was hung and a painter then decorated it. Walls were also hung with ornamental leather.

Carpets and tea were not the only signs of the influence of eastern trade to be seen in the homes of Englishmen. Lacquered furniture, either imported from China or copied from Chinese models, was popular and walls were decorated with Chinese wallpapers. But one always has to remember that the new fashions only affected a small proportion of the population. Country cottages and the houses of industrial workers in the towns were still simply furnished with fairly rough materials. When Tom Jones was refused a bed at a country inn he 'very contentedly betook himself to a great chair made with rushes'.

These great differences in standards observed by different classes of people are also evident in the case of food.

Fielding's food

Fielding fed well but not luxuriously. This is also true, on the whole, of his characters. He was slightly priggish about the French dishes which were now to be had in certain elegant St. James's restaurants. Not for him their perigord-pie (pie with truffles), their ortolans (small succulent birds, like larks), their turtles or their custards. These, he wrote, 'will never convey happiness to the heart or cheerfulness to the countenance'. A good appetite, in Fielding's view, was the best sauce.

During the voyage to Lisbon (Chapter VIII), the ship put in at a number of channel ports where fresh food was to be had. The Fieldings bought their own food and had a chest of tea with them. They ate roast beef, roast mutton, beans, bacon and venison (roast or baked). One meal which they particularly enjoyed consisted of soles, whitings and lobsters. They were fond of cream. The ladies went ashore one day and were given it with their afternoon tea at an ale-house.

When the ship was off Devon the Fieldings bought clotted cream and butter, and a fish called a John Dorée, like turbot but firmer and tastier. The captain was

Instructions from *The Country Housewife and Lady's Director in the Management of a House* (1732), written, not by a woman, but by Richard Bradley, Professor of Botany in the University of Cambridge and Fellow of the Royal Society.

The Manner of Truſſing a ſingle Rabbit *for Roaſting. From Mr.*W.N.*Poulterer.*

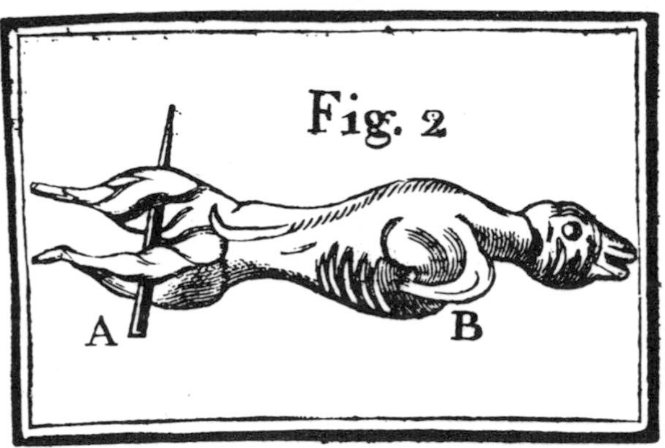

YOU caſe the Rabbit all, excepting the lower Joints of the four Legs, and thoſe you chop off: then paſs a Skewer through the middle of the Haunches, after you have laid them flat, as at A; and the Fore-Legs, which are called the Wings, muſt be turn'd, as at B; ſo that the ſmaller Joint

thought to be fond of sheep's-head broth. Once the ship was out of reach of the land the food was much simpler. Most of the passengers were anyway too seasick to eat. But when a shark was caught, the crew enjoyed the stew of salt beef and shark meat which was served.

Towards the end of the voyage Fielding lamented the lack of fresh food. His party had no bread left, only ship's biscuit. The fact that they still had 'a great number of old ducks and fowls' (alive), seems not to have afforded them much comfort.

Tom Jones's food

Tom Jones shared his creator's liking for plain food. After hunting with Squire Western he had roast beef. When recovering from being hit over the head with a bottle he 'swallowed a large mess of chicken broth, with a pound of bacon into the bargain'. For breakfast next day he had tea and two pieces of buttered toast, after which he slept for seven hours. When he woke he was hungry and a piece of cold buttock (beef) and carrot were fried for him. On a later occasion we find him 'falling to' on 'an excellent, smoaking dish of eggs and bacon' ('smoaking' simply means hot, not burnt). He liked eggs in the plural. One day he had nothing but one poached egg all morning, with the result that he felt badly in need of the roast mutton which was provided at the next inn. He could eat the larger half of a shoulder of mutton at one meal.

Sophia's and Moll's food

When Sophia was being kept in her room by her father, to prevent her from seeing Tom Jones, she was nevertheless allowed the best of food. She was very fond of pullets', partridges' and pheasants' eggs. A chicken was brought up for her dinner. Inside, where we now put stuffing, it was full of her favourite eggs. However, concealed among the eggs was a letter from Jones. So eggs and chicken had to wait till the letter was read.

Moll Flanders was another person who liked chicken. A woman who had taken a fancy to her sent a maid along with meals. One day there was a roast chicken and a bottle of sherry. Next day the maid heated some chocolate for Moll's breakfast and returned at noon with 'the sweetbread of a breast of veal, whole, and a dish of soup'. Moll seldom had it so good. There is little about food or drink in her story, but she once paid a visit to an alehouse for professional reasons, viz. in order to steal one of the silver tankards, and, since the morning was cold, she ordered a pint of warm ale.

Simple food

Parson Adams and Joseph Andrews ate very simply. A large loaf, cheese and a pitcher of beer could be like a feast to them. Fielding once more takes the opportunity of pointing out that their appetites were much better than 'are to be found at the most exquisite eating-houses in the parish of St. James's'. Although their adventures may be imagined as taking place about 1740, by which time tea was by no means confined to the rich, they still sometimes had ale with their toast for breakfast, and Adams, breakfasting with his wife, ate bacon and cabbage. At Lady Booby's, on the other hand, the company at breakfast drank tea. The two best meals recorded in the book are the picnic, when Joseph and Adams enjoyed a cold fowl and a bottle of wine, and the wedding feast, when Adams was filled with ale and pudding.

Pudding

'Pudding' then as now was a word used to describe various dishes, both sweet and savoury. A visiting Frenchman wrote that no Sunday dinner was complete without it, to accompany 'a huge piece of Roast Beef, of which they stuff till they can swallow no more.' But what was pudding made of? The same Frenchman wrote:

> The Pudding is a Dish very difficult to be describ'd, because of the several Sorts there are of it: Flower [flour], Milk, Eggs, Butter, Sugar, Suet, Marrow from bones, Raisins, etc., are the most common Ingredients of a Pudding. They bake them in an Oven, they boil them with Meat, they make them fifty several Ways: BLESSED BE HE THAT INVENTED PUDDING.

Mealtimes

The shopkeeper whose day is described on p. 193 dined at noon. This was in 1706. As the century advanced, dinner times became later. Two o'clock was usual, but fashionable people might wait till four. A former man of fashion told Parson Adams that he had spent his afternoons and evenings as follows:

2 – 4 dressed myself
4 – 6 dined
6 – 8 coffee-house
8 – 9 Drury-lane playhouse
9 – 10 Lincoln's Inn Fields
10 – 12 Drawing-room

Lady Bellaston must have dined about the same time, since she wrote to Tom Jones: 'Come to me exactly at seven; I dine abroad [out] but will be at home by that time.'

A man of fashion might go to a coffee house after dinner, but in a private house coffee was not usually served. The men were left drinking wine and later joined the ladies for tea and biscuits. Supper, then as now, might be anything from an evening snack to an elegant meal eaten during a ball in the early hours of the morning. Breakfast was usually a light meal of tea and toast or bread; it was not always taken immediately after getting up. A cup of chocolate was sometimes drunk first thing in the morning. As we have seen, Adams liked bacon and cabbage for breakfast, and the Winchester boys, whose diet is given on p. 98, had beef or mutton broth.

Porridge

The list of vegetables ordered for Blenheim (p. 52) shows the variety which was available. Many market gardens had been established near London and other big towns. But poorer people ate few vegetables, except potatoes, and often had meatless days. Porridge and oatcakes were their stand-by, though the porridge might be made with milk. Three Sheffield apprentices who were given 'grout porridge' for supper—porridge made with water and the refuse of grain which had already been used for brewing—threw it on their master's fire. He beat them, but afterwards the porridge improved, possibly even deserving the name 'Hasty Pudding', which was porridge made with butter, milk or treacle. It appears, as a Saturday night treat, on the following list of meals served to children at the Foundling Hospital (1747):

	Breakfast	Dinner	Supper
Sunday	Broth	Roast Pork	Bread
Monday	Gruell	Potatoes	Milk and Bread
Tuesday	Milk Porridge	Boiled Mutton	Bread
Wednesday	Broth	Rice Milk	Bread and Cheese
Thursday	Gruell	Boiled Pork	Bread
Friday	Milk Porridge	Dumplins	Milk and Bread
Saturday	Gruell	Hasty Puddings	Bread and Cheese

It was, however, enacted that the diet of the staff should be as follows:

Upon Sundays Roast Beef, Mondays Stew'd Beef with Turneps and Carrotts, Tuesdays Roast Mutton, Wednesdays Boil'd Beef with Greens or Roots, or Pork with Pease Pudding in Winter, or Shoulders of Veal in Summer, Thursdays Stew'd Beef with Turneps and Carrotts, Fridays Roast Mutton, and Saturdays Boiled Beef with Greens or Roots, or Pork with Pease Pudding in Winter and Shoulders of Veal in Summer. And that the Proportion of the said Diet be at present Regulated at a Pound for each Head a Day . . . And, That the Breakfasts and Suppers be Milk Porridge, Rice Milk or Bread and Cheese.

Tea

Tea does not appear in the above lists. It had first reached England, together with coffee and chocolate, towards the middle of the seventeenth century. It was then drunk, as the Chinese drink it, without milk or sugar. In the first half of the eighteenth century tea became much more popular than chocolate or coffee. It was taken with milk or cream and sugar (which by that time was no longer a rare luxury); but it was not yet firmly established as the national drink. Men have

Tea chest designed by Chippendale.

always been less fond of it than women and today might still prefer a beer-break to a tea-break, were it not for the restricted hours during which alcohol can be sold. There was also opposition to tea on grounds of health. John Wesley was convinced that tea-drinking affected his nerves and made his hand shake. He first tried taking it weaker, with more milk and sugar, but finally gave it up altogether. In 1748 he provided the following breakfast suggestions for those who found that tea disagreed with them:

1. Take half a Pint of Milk every Morning, with a little Bread, not boiled, but warmed only; (a Man in tolerable Health might double the Quantity.)
2. If this is too heavy, add as much Water, and boil it together with a Spoonful of Oatmeal.
3. If this agrees not, try half a Pint, or a little more, of Water-gruel, neither thick nor thin; not sweetened (for that may be apt to make you sick) but with a very little Butter, Salt, and Bread.
4. If this disagrees, try Sage, green Balm, Mint, or Pennyroyal Tea, infusing only so much of the Herb as just to change the Colour of the Water.
5. Try two or three of these mixed, in various Proportions.
6. Try ten or twelve other *English* herbs.
7. Try *Foltron,* a Mixture of Herbs to be had at many Grocers, far healthier as well as cheaper than Tea.
8. Try Coco.

   If after having tried each of these for a Week or ten Days, you find none of them well agree with your Constitution, then use . . . Tea again: But at the same Time know, That your having used it so long, has brought you near the Chambers of Death.

Milk

Cheese and butter were brought to the towns from distant parts of the country. Cheeses were beginning to be known by their place of origin and a London

A tea-party in the 1720's. The cups have no handles. The tea-pot is on a stand, and the tea caddy is beside the elbow of the girl on the left. There are tongs for taking sugar; teaspoons for stirring it are shown on a dish, not in individual saucers. The jug is probably for hot water, though it may have been for hot milk, which was beginning to be added to tea in England about this time. Later in the century cold milk or cream was used.

tavern which still exists had been called the 'Cheshire Cheese'. But milk could not be transported great distances. It could not be transported even for short distances without getting dirty or being deliberately adulterated. It was safer to move the cow or donkey with the milk still inside her. (Donkey milk is good for invalids and young children.) Prudent householders bought from roundsmen who brought their animals to the door and served each customer direct from the udder. Even then the cow might be dirty and ill-nourished. To be quite sure of a really good drink, it was best to get it from one of the cows which grazed in St. James's Park.

Beer and Wine

Beer, under which head I include ale and porter (p. 161), was still the favourite drink of most people. Men, women and children drank it, hot, or cold, at all times of the day. Gin became a dangerous rival to it for some years. It is dealt with on p. 207, at the end of 'Fun' just before 'Trouble' begins.

Some alcoholic drinks were made by housewives, as they are today, e.g., elderberry wine, currant gin or cherry brandy; but few vines were grown. Almost all the wine, which was drunk in large quantities with and after meals by the middle and upper classes, came from abroad. During Marlborough's wars, when the French

A painting by Hogarth of gentlemen drinking wine. Glasses are cone-shaped. Bottles are rounder than those of today. On the left is a wine-cooler, probably made of silver and containing ice. A fresh bottle is being lifted out of it.

Gout.

were our enemies, French wines did not disappear from the table. Some were captured at sea and some were smuggled in. But they were not so easy to get as they had been and wines from other countries became more popular.

Wines from Portugal had a special advantage after the Methuen Treaty (1703) in which it was agreed that Portugal would allow the import of English cloth, while England would lower the duty payable on Portuguese wine. As a result the English gentleman who drank Port (called after Oporto, in Portugal, whence it was shipped) or Madeira (called after one of the Canary Islands, ruled by Portugal, whence it came), not only got a bargain; he could also feel patriotic. He was stimulating the English cloth trade, in which, if there were sheep on his land, he had a direct interest, and he was injuring the trade of England's chief rival, France. He therefore drank a great deal of port. Three or four bottles could go down one throat in an evening. But the price of patriotism might be an attack of gout, which began with excruciating pain in the big toe during the early hours of the morning. Jacobites, who loved France and therefore drank claret, slept better.

An 18th century man's suit, now in the London Museum. It is of fawn-coloured brocade with deep cuffs and silk-covered buttons. The figure holds a malacca 'cane' (a word then applied to any thick walking stick).

Close-up of brocade and buttons on the suit above.

What did they wear?

Port-drinking Whigs or claret-drinking Jacobites, they and their wives all wore the same kind of clothes in bed—a loose-fitting night-shirt and a close-fitting cap. Humbler folk, including Parson Adams, wore nothing or did not bother to undress.

'Nightgowns' were what we would call dressing-gowns—worn, together with a soft, pointed cap, when you first got up, until it was time to put on more formal clothes—but some men did not bother to change out of their nightgowns before paying the first visit of the day to a coffee house.

It was compulsory to be buried in a woollen shroud, in order to benefit the wool industry, but woollen underclothes were not yet worn. A linen shirt, trimmed with lace at the neck and cuffs, and underpants were the basic garments of a man. Next he would put on his breeches, stockings—more than one pair if the weather were cold—and shoes. Stockings, which sometimes overlapped the breeches above the knee but were held up by garters tied below it, could be brightly coloured and elegantly embroidered. Shoes, since the reign of William and Mary, had had buckles instead of bows and sometimes rather high red heels.

Bows and buttons

Since there was no elastic, garters were simply pieces of ribbon or material tied in a bow, as they had been for centuries. But the eighteenth century gentleman had fewer bows to tie than his Elizabethan ancestor; an unusual fastening device had become popular—the button.

Buttons were not a new invention. They had been used, for instance, at Ur of the Chaldees (where a skeleton was found with a row of fifteen down its chest) and in ancient Crete. But they did not become a common part of English clothes until manufacture of them began in Birmingham during the seventeenth century.

Baths and shaving

With our gentleman already half dressed it is clear that he is not going to have a bath this morning. Louis XIV, whose court set the fashion for all Europe, was said to have a bath once a year and there is no reason to suppose that in those days the English were any more interested in personal cleanliness than the

French. Tom Jones stayed at many inns during his travels and became involved in numerous rows with inn-keepers and their servants, but never about water for washing. Fielding had many complaints about conditions on board the ship which took him to Lisbon, but the difficulty of keeping clean did not worry him.

Though he did not have a bath, our gentleman may have washed. As we have seen, Chippendale was designing wash-stands by the middle of the century. Soap was not only imported, but also manufactured in England and made at home. It was sometimes spherical in shape and called a 'wash-ball'. Shaving might be done by a footman or could wait until it was convenient to visit the barber; but Chippendale assumed that some of his clients would shave themselves, since he designed a 'shaving table' with racks for razors and a movable mirror.

How much of the face had to be shaved? The whole of it. Throughout the eighteenth century all gentlemen were clean-shaven. More than that. They also shaved

A wig-powdering 'carrot' in use. It is of rosewood. The powder is ejected through a nozzle at the thin end. (Meanwhile a servant robs his master's desk.) Powdering was sometimes done in 'closets' (p. 86).

their heads; for the eighteenth was the century of wigs as well as Whigs.

Wigs

'Wig' is short for 'periwig', from the French *perruque*. The word came into use towards the end of the seventeenth century when the wearing of wigs by gentlemen had become normal practice. Wigs, like buttons, had been worn by certain people since ancient times. Queen Elizabeth wore one to conceal baldness when she grew old. At the time of writing they are becoming fashionable among younger women who have plenty of their own hair. But only between the reigns of Charles II and George III have wigs been more or less obligatory for all respectable men.

I say 'more or less', because John Wesley, for instance, wore his own long hair. There was once a distressing scene when his wife seized hold of it in one of her tantrums and dragged him round the room. Wig-wearers were spared this particular indignity; but they ran other risks. Thieves had been known to cut a hole in the hood of a closed carriage and steal off travellers' heads the wigs which had perhaps cost them as much as £30. But the big 'full-bottomed' wigs resembling those now worn by judges, gave place towards the middle of the century to smaller wigs similar to those now worn by barristers.

Bewigged, in shirt, breeches and stockings, a man had only to put on a lace cravat (a cross between a scarf and a tie), a waistcoat and a coat, both reaching almost to the knees, to be fully dressed for indoors. Before going out, in Queen Anne's reign, he would put on a sword; but this practice was gradually dropped under the Hanoverians. He carried a three-cornered hat, but often did not wear it because of the size of his wig. He also carried a stout but elegant cane and wore a cloak, if the

Lady, nurse and child—dolls of about 1730 with wooden heads and bodies. The lady is in blue silk and, surprisingly, wears no cap; the nurse wears a brown silk jacket-bodice and skirt; the contents of her pockets are described on p. 85. The child is dressed like a miniature adult.

weather made it necessary. Accessories such as snuff-box, watch, handkerchief and purse were now carried in pockets, a convenience invented by tailors about 1670.

No handbags

Women too had pockets. These were tied on separately over the petticoat and were reached through slits in the skirt. They were elegantly embroidered and held handkerchiefs or love-letters. Sometimes they might also contain a snuff-box, or a box of small black patches of different shapes and sizes with which women then decorated their faces. In the pockets of the female doll (p. 84) were found a handkerchief, a 'housewife' (small sewing outfit) and a pincushion. Pins were needed to keep clothes in place. Women had not yet taken to buttons.

Make-up equipment was less portable than it is today and was usually confined to the bedroom. Handbags were therefore not carried.

Because the crowded and littered town streets were evil-smelling, women sometimes sniffed at a pungent kind of incense which was carried in a little silver box with holes in the lid. This was known as a 'casolette'. Towards the end of the century, a chemist invented a powerful infusion of herbs and spices in glacial acetic acid. This was believed to be a protection against infection as well as bad smells and a sponge soaked in it was carried by men and women alike in containers called 'vinaigrettes'.

Shifts and skirts

No pants or brassières were worn. (Even if brassières had been known, the neck-line would have been too low to make them wearable.) The basic garment was a shift or shirt not unlike a man's. Those who were not content with the body provided for them by nature wore corsets over the shift. These were laced up the back, starting from the waist, so that the breasts were pushed upwards.

Hooped skirts came in during Queen Anne's reign and grew wider, as the Elizabethan farthingale had done. By 1730 these skirts were six feet in diameter, making it difficult for two women to sit side by side in a coach. The hoops were of whalebone, sewn into the petticoat or into the skirt itself. Fielding wrote a contemptuous article about them. Doubtless for this reason his heroine Fanny, in *Joseph Andrews*, wore for her wedding 'nothing richer than a white dimity [stout cotton cloth] nightgown'. This was worn over a shift with an edging of lace round the bosom and a pair of fine white thread stockings. On her head she wore a cap 'and over it a little straw hat, lined with cherry-coloured silk, and tied with a cherry-coloured ribbon'.

Moll Flanders also dressed simply, if the theft she was planning made it necessary. For stealing luggage at an inn where stage-coaches started, she wore 'an ordinary stuff gown, a blue apron, and a straw hat'.

Hair styles

Women were not prepared to shave off their hair and depend entirely on wigs, as men were doing, but fashionable ladies might have other hair mixed with their own, particularly in the complicated styles of Queen Anne's reign, when hair was piled high round a wire framework called a *commode* and topped with an elaborate lace cap.

Powdering of the hair or wig was important for both sexes and in houses of the period you can still find 'powder-closets' (like small rooms or big cupboards) where ladies and gentlemen once sat in dust cloaks, sometimes holding stiff paper cones, like dunces' caps, over their faces, while their heads were powdered and perfumed (picture on p. 82).

Stockings, hats and accessories

Women's stockings, gartered below the knee like those of men, were of all colours, until about 1737, when white became fashionable. At her wedding (see above – it would have been in the 1740's) even Fanny wore white stockings. The fashion was condemned as immoral, white being considered only one remove from nudity, but it persisted. Anyhow no one except the wearer saw very much of the stockings, unless by accident.

A fan was the commonest accessory, and there was a wide variety of jewellery. Like men, women wore cloaks out of doors in cold or rainy weather. These were fitted with hoods. Hats were varied. Fanny's, for her wedding, and Moll's for her thieving have already been mentioned.

Umbrellas

Parasols to keep off the sun had been introduced from the East and a similar device was beginning to be used to keep off the rain. This came to be called an 'umbrella' (in spite of the fact that the word comes from the Latin 'umbra', meaning shade). Though used by women in our period it had not become an elegant accessory. To carry one was an admission that you could not afford a coach or a sedan chair. Men thought umbrellas effeminate. Not till about 1750 did the London merchant Jonas Hanway use one regularly in public and umbrellas were not generally accepted by men until later in the century.

Children's clothes

Children were dressed like their elders, except that boys did not wear wigs. Babies, however, had special long clothes and nappies. This brings us to the next chapter, which is about being born and growing up.

This baby doll (about 1730), of ›od, wears a nappy under an ivory ›tin dress.

CHAPTER III

GROWING UP

HOW MUCH did it cost to be born? Most babies were born at home, but on one of the occasions when Moll Flanders was expecting she went to a kind of small maternity home, where three scales of charges were in operation. She chose the cheapest, as follows:

	£. s. d.
1. For three months' lodging, including diet, at 10s. a week	6. 0. 0.
2. For a nurse for the month and use of child-bed linen	1. 10. 0.
3. For a minister to christen the child, etc.	1. 10. 0.
4. Supper for mother and five friends at the christening	1. 0. 0.
5. Midwife's fee, etc.	3. 3. 0.
6. Maidservant's fee	10. 0.
	13. 13. 0.

'Then madam,' the woman in charge cheerfully explained, 'if the child should not live, as it sometimes happens, there is the minister's payment saved; and if you have no friends to come, you may save the expense of a supper.'

Vital statistics

'If the child should not live.' What are called 'vital statistics'—statistics referring to births and deaths—were

18th century feeding bottle for babies. It is made of pewter.

not accurately collected until the nineteenth century, but estimates have been made. According to one of these 74.5% of all children christened between 1730 and 1749 were buried before they turned five. Nor were these all natural deaths. 'No expedient has yet been found out', we read, 'for preventing murders of poor miserable infants at their birth, or for suppressing the inhuman custom of exposing newly-born infants to perish in the streets.'

How the Wesleys were brought up

If you survived, what sort of upbringing could you expect? The mother of John Wesley wrote down at his request the rules she had observed in educating her family. During their first months her children were rocked in their cradles while they slept, three hours in the morning and three in the afternoon. This daytime sleep was gradually reduced till none was needed. Then, 'when turned a year old, (and some before) they were taught to fear the rod'.

There were three meals a day, at which behaviour was strict. Drinking or eating between meals was never allowed. 'At six, as soon as family-prayer was over, they had their supper; at seven, the maid washed them; and, beginning at the youngest, she undressed and got them all to bed by eight.'

As soon as they could speak, the children were taught the Lord's Prayer, then other prayers and verses from the Bible. They learned to read at five and from then on there were six hours of lessons every day—nine to twelve and two to five.

How Moll Flanders was brought up

Moll Flanders, who had no parents, was less strictly brought up. She had the good fortune to be boarded with a kindly woman who kept a little school where reading, spinning and needlework were taught. When she was eight she would normally have been sent away to become a domestic servant. She managed to argue herself out of this and stayed until she was fourteen; but during those years she was earning her keep by

Epworth Old Rectory, the home of the Wesleys.

One way of starting life. Women draw lots, each hoping to obtain a place for her child at the Foundling Hospital (1749).

spinning and sewing, so she cannot have had very much time for study.

Lady Mary Wortley Montagu

There was no compulsory schooling in the eighteenth century and even people who could afford to pay for schooling did not necessarily provide it for their children. The mother of Lady Mary Wortley Montagu (1689-1762) died while Mary was still a child. Her father gave her the use of his library and a friend of the family, who was a bishop, gave her some help in learning Latin. Yet she became an accomplished letter-writer and one of the leading figures of the eighteenth century. Her son was not allowed the same degree of freedom. He was sent to Winchester. But he ran away twice, after which he was made to travel with a tutor in the West Indies.

When she became a grandmother, Lady Mary wrote several letters of advice on how the grandchildren were to be brought up. Her daughter's eldest girl turned out

Alexander Pope, in the cap and loose-fitting 'nightgown' which men wore on informal occasions indoors.

to be intelligent. She was particularly good at arithmetic. Lady Mary thought that she should be encouraged in her studies. 'No entertainment is so cheap as reading, nor any pleasure so lasting.' The girl should learn Latin and Greek but not think herself learned for doing so. Lady Mary went on:

> Languages are more properly to be called vehicles of learning than learning itself. True knowledge consists in knowing things, not words. I would wish her no further a linguist than to enable her to read books in their originals, that are often corrupted, and always injured, by translations. Two hours application every morning will bring this about much sooner than you can imagine, and she will have leisure enough besides to run over the English poetry, which is a more important part of a woman's education than it is generally supposed.

However, Lady Mary felt that the girl should be warned to conceal her learning, for

> the parade of it can only serve to draw on her the envy, and consequently the most inveterate hatred, of all he and she fools, which will certainly be at least three parts in four of all her acquaintance.

Pope's short schooldays

Alexander Pope (1688-1744) was another person of distinction whose education was irregular. He was a delicate child and learned little before he was eight, when a tutor started him on Greek and Latin. He next went to a country boarding school. There he was flogged for impertinence. The flogging of boys went on pretty consistently in every century until the twentieth. Most parents flogged their children themselves and had no objection to schoolmasters doing so. But Pope's parents were different. They immediately removed their son from his school and sent him to a gentler one in London. Here he wrote a play, based on Homer's *Iliad,* which was performed by the boys and the school gardener. But at the age of twelve he left school for good, lived at home and educated himself.

Hogarth illustrates his exercise book

William Hogarth (1697-1764), son of an unsuccessful schoolmaster and author, decided at an early age that he would do better to concentrate on drawing than on learning from books. 'My exercises when at school', he wrote, 'were more remarkable for the ornaments [i.e. the drawings which adorned them], than for the exercise itself. In the former [the exercises], I soon found that blockheads with better memories could much surpass me; but for the latter I was particularly distinguished.' He left school as early as he could and became apprenticed to an engraver.

The Reverend Mr. Thwackum

Fielding's Tom Jones was far from being a delicate, intellectual or artistic child, but he too was not sent to

Thwackum, played by Peter Bull.

school. Tom's guardian, having noted the many vices which boys acquired at 'public schools' (see p. 99), preferred to employ tutors at home. Since 'home' in this case was an estate in Gloucestershire, you might think Tom's lot enviable, and he certainly managed to lead an adventurous life. But since Mr. Thwackum, the principal tutor, 'a fellow of a college, with a great reputation for learning, religion and sobriety of manners', had only one other boy to instruct and to flog, he was able to concentrate on Tom to an extent which Tom found burdensome.

Flogging horse and birch at the school in Lichfield which Johnson attended. They disappeared when the building was demolished (1849).

Eton

Tom Jones's guardian was not the only Fielding character who hated 'public schools'. 'The nurseries of all vice and immorality', Parson Adams calls them in *Joseph Andrews,* adding, 'All the wicked fellows whom I remember at the university were bred at them.' However, Fielding himself went to Eton and has recorded no complaint about the life there.

Boys with a taste for writing were not necessarily unhappy at school. Dr. Samuel Johnson attributed his accurate knowledge of Latin to the ferocious headmaster of Lichfield School, who would say, as he beat a boy, 'And this I do to save you from the gallows.' The Doctor shared the headmaster's belief in beating knowledge into children and sin out of them; so, although he was from time to time a victim himself, he bore the school no grudge.

Horace Walpole (1717-1797), son of the first Prime Minister and writer of even more letters than Lady Mary Wortley Montagu, remained deeply attached to Eton, where he had made lasting friendships. A number of old Etonians had already formed the habit of dining together in London once a year. But they went first to church to hear a sermon.

Fielding was at Eton during the early 1720's. The date of his leaving is not known. It must have been before November 1725, by which time he was eighteen and making love to an heiress in Dorset. The numbers in the school were then around 400. They varied according to the prosperity of the wealthier classes of society. Before the South Sea Bubble (1720) they had risen to 425; in the following year they were down to 375. Here is a bill which shows the cost of keeping William Pitt, later Lord Chatham, at Eton for half a year. Young Pitt must have had an accident and the surgeon who was called got as much for his visit as poor Mr. Good for half a year's teaching. Of course Good had more than one pupil. Classes, of which there were ten at this time, contained between 25 and 50 boys; and there were ten masters, including the Headmaster, to take charge of them.

Mr Clarks Receipt to make Ink

Take 4 ounces of ye best blue galls bruis'd, ~~[illegible]~~
of Copperas. One ounce of Gum Arabick, put them into
one Quart of Spring Water. ye more you shake ye
Bottle ye better. — put alittle salt in to keep it from moulding
Note if you put too much Copperas in, it eats ye paper, alittle Brandy keeps
it from Freezing

Here then is:

Mr. William Pitt, his Bill. 1719.

	£	s.	d.
Paid at the House where Mr. William was when he fell down		13.	6.
paid a man and horse to go with me		3.	0.
paid for a shaze [chaise—a light carriage]		5.	0.
To the surgeon for attendance, bleeding, etc.	2.	2.	0.
To the other surgeon for going to visit him	1.	1.	0.
2 pairs of stockings		6.	6.
paid for curing his chilblanes		5.	0.
Fire money to the Master		1.	6.
School sweeping 8d., chapell 4d., water 3d.		1.	3.
Share of fire in his Chamber to Easter		10.	0.
6 pound of candles		3.	6.
a pair of garters			4.
Halfe a year's cleaning shooes to Midsummer		5.	0.
Worstead and thread to mend his Linnen and stockings		1.	0.
Hatter's Bill		1.	8.
Barber, a Quarter		7.	6.
Taylor's bill		3.	6.
Shoomaker's bill		19.	6.
Bookseller's bill	1.	11.	6.
Writing master halfe a year August 7th	1.	2.	0.
To Mr. Burchet halfe a year's Tuition	4.	4.	0.
To Mr. Good halfe a years Teaching	2.	2.	0.
For halfe a years board due August 7th, 1719	12.	10.	0.
	29.	0.	3.

Opposite A gardener's handwriting, *c.* 1750.
Mr Clearks Receipt to make Ink. Take 4 ounces of ye best blue galls bruis'd, 1 ounce & ½ of Copperas, One ounce of Gum Arabick, put them into one Quart of Spring Water, ye more ye shake ye Bottle ye better—put a little salt in to keep it from moalding.
Note if you put too much Copper in, it eats ye paper, a little Brandy keeps it from freezing.

Towards the beginning of the eighteenth century the seventy scholars of Winchester College were put on an improved ration scale. Previously they had only had hot meat on Sundays. On Fridays and Saturdays, which had been fast days in the Middle Ages, there had been only bread for breakfast, followed by a bread, butter and cheese lunch and, on Fridays, no supper at all. The new menus were as follows and each of the three meals was accompanied by a pint of beer and half a pound of bread for each scholar.

Sunday	Breakfast	Beef-broth
	Dinner	Roast beef
	Supper	Boiled mutton without broth
Monday	Breakfast	Mutton broth saved from Sunday night
	Dinner	Boiled beef hot, without broth
	Supper	Boiled mutton and broth
Tuesday	Breakfast	Beef broth saved from Monday

and so on, each day the same, until

Friday	Breakfast	Beef broth saved from Thursday
	Dinner	Baked pudding made of flour, bread, fruit, spice, milk and butter
	Supper	Boiled mutton without broth
Saturday	Breakfast	Mutton broth saved from Friday
	Dinner	Baked pudding
	Supper	Boiled mutton and broth

All this food may or may not have helped to attract scholars to the College. Certainly their number remained a steady seventy. On the other hand the number of commoners (non-scholars whose parents paid), varied. There were, for example, 49 commoners in 1702, but only 20 in 1717; there were 93 in 1737, but only 10 in 1750. The low figures for 1717 and 1750 may be partly due to the aftermath of the 1715 and 1745 Jacobite rebellions. The college was known to favour the Stuarts, so much so that on the anniversary of the accession of

George I in 1718, some of the boys attended the service of celebration in the cathedral dressed as though they were attending a funeral. The Secretary of State (there was not yet a Prime Minister) wrote ordering that they should be whipped. This kind of minor scandal may well have discouraged any but fanatically Jacobite parents from sending their boys to Winchester.

Public Schools

Like Winchester, Eton was tainted with Jacobitism. This fact, combined with the efforts of an energetic and influential Whig governor, set the Grammar School founded in 1571 by John Lyon at Harrow on the road to fame. At the beginning of the eighteenth century the terms 'public school' and 'grammar school' were both used to denote any school with endowments and a governing body, as opposed to a private school run by one person; but a distinction between better and less known schools was already recognized. Defoe in 1728 referred to 'the great schools of Eton, Winchester, Westminster, Felsted, Bishop Stortford, Canterbury and others'. Harrow now became one of these.

Grammar Schools

The Grammar School at Andover was in a flourishing state. Boarders were so numerous in 1732 that the Schoolhouse became too small for them. Shrewsbury School, however, was passing through a bad period. Numbers were low and, in the words of a former pupil, the school was 'in low repute and the Chief Schoolmaster at that time by his age and infirmities rendered incapable to discharge his duty'. The fact that Liverpool Grammar School was given a new set of rules in 1748, suggests that here too all had not been well during the first half of the eighteenth century. The Headmaster was now ordered to teach Latin and English, and to keep a register of attendance and offences. The under-master was to teach reading, writing and arithmetic. Both masters were to attend school in summer from 7 a.m. to 12.0 and from 2 p.m. to 5 p.m., and in winter from 8 a.m.. to 12.0 and 1.30 to 4 p.m. Holidays were to be three weeks at Christmas, one at Easter and a fortnight at Whitsun.

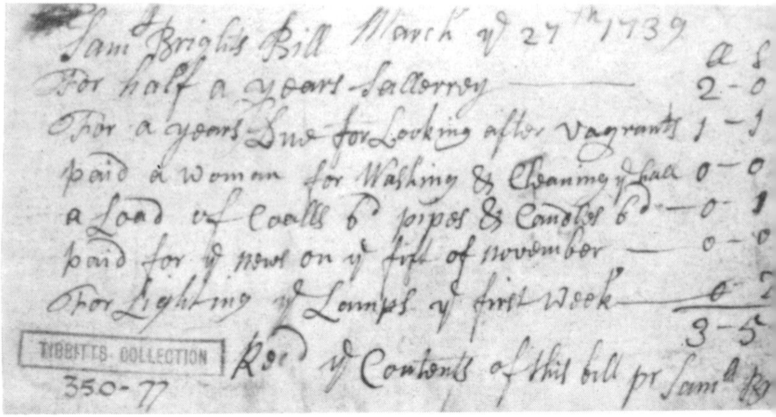
Saml Brights Bill March ye 27th 1739 £ s
For half a years Sallorry — 2-0
For a years Due for Looking after Vagrants 1-
paid a Woman for Washing & Cleaning ye hall 0-0
a Load of Coalls 6d pipes & Candles 6d — 0-1
paid for ye news on ye fift of november — 0-0
For Lighting ye Lamps ye first week — 0-
3-5
Recd ye Contents of this bill pr Saml Br
TIBBITTS COLLECTION
350-77

Sam Bright was the caretaker of Sheffield Town Hall. He had learned to write, but his spelling of 'salary' (line 2) is unusual.

At Newcastle the year 1749 was a turning point. The Free Grammar School of Queen Elizabeth, after a period during which it had been almost empty, now received one of its greatest headmasters, who stayed for thirty-eight years and re-established the school's reputation.

If the Free Grammar School at Newcastle was almost empty and other schools of repute all over the country had declined, for various reasons, during the first half of the eighteenth century, where did boys get their education? As noted above, richer parents often preferred to engage tutors and small private schools were also available. But the tutors and private schools did not necessarily provide a more interesting curriculum. Some boys, like Hogarth (p. 93), found a solution in apprenticeship. Captain Cook, the explorer, began his sea career by becoming an apprentice in a firm of Whitby shipowners at the age of twelve.

Nonconformist academies

Some of the 'public schools' in coastal towns and in London (e.g. Dartmouth Grammar School and Christ's Hospital) introduced the teaching of mathematics and navigation; but an unconventional curriculum (i.e. one not consisting mainly of Latin and Greek) could often be found only in schools run by nonconformists—people who did not *conform* to Church of England beliefs and whose children were therefore not admitted to the 'public schools' nor to Oxford or Cambridge—the only two English universities at the time. At these nonconformist academies, as they were called, a wide range of subjects could be studied. At one such academy in London, which John Wesley's father and Daniel Defoe attended, French, Italian, Spanish, mathematics, science, history, geography, logic and politics were taught, as well as the normal Greek and Latin. When John Wesley founded Kingswood School, Bath, for Methodists in 1748, the curriculum was similar to the above, with the addition of Hebrew, metaphysics and ethics.

But an unconventional curriculum did not mean, as it might nowadays, unconventional discipline. Kingswood, for children of 12-16, was stricter than other schools. The hours were 4.0 a.m. to 8.0 p.m. The children seldom had tea or coffee, there were two meatless days a week and Friday was a fast day until 3.0 p.m. Play was forbidden. The children were supposed to get their exercise by chopping wood, digging in the garden and drawing water.

To the majority of parents the question of broadening the curriculum was of no interest. They could not even read or write. What chance existed for their children to learn to do so? Not much. In the first place most parents needed the labour or the earnings of their children from about the age of seven. Secondly, there was no general feeling that every child in the country should have some education. It was felt that the more one learned the more discontented one was likely to become, and that an ignorant worker was likely to be less discontented than one who had begun to develop wider interests. This problem of how much education people need is still with us, but it has moved a couple of steps higher. The question today is: Who ought to go to the university?

In spite of the arguments against educating poor people, it was felt in Queen Anne's reign that something should be done for them. 'Charity schools', paid for by public subscription or by wealthy benefactors, were gradually established throughout the country to teach what one might call the four R's—Reading, wRiting, aRithmetic and Religion—to poor children aged between seven and twelve.

Slates and slate pencils were used for rough work. Quills, made from the wing-feathers of geese, swans, peacocks or crows, were still the most usual type of pen. Lead pencils were not yet common, though Marlborough (p. 49) used one.

In Newcastle, four charity schools were set up in connection with the town's four churches. The boys were taught reading, writing and how to keep accounts, the girls knitting, sewing, reading and sometimes writing and arithmetic. Each year the children were supplied with footwear and a uniform, the colour of which varied

WOMAN

Not Inferior to

MAN:

OR,

A ſhort and modeſt Vindication of the natural Right of the *Fair-Sex* to a perfect Equality of Power, Dignity, and Eſteem, with the Men.

By *SOPHIA*,
A Person of Quality.

How hard is the Condition of our Sex,
Thro' ev'ry State of Life the Slaves of Man?

--------------- *Wherefore are we*
Born with high Souls, but to aſſert ourſelves,
Shake off this wild Obedience they exact,
And claim an equal Empire in the World.
Rowe's Fair Penitent.

LONDON:

Printed for Jacob Robinson, at the *Golden-Lion* in *Ludgate-Street.* M.DCC.XLIII.

[Price One Shilling.]

A plea for the rights of women (1743).

MAN

SUPERIOR TO

WOMAN:

OR, THE

Natural Right of the Men

TO

Sovereign Authority over the Women,
Aſſerted and Defended.

BEING AN

ANSWER

To that celebrated Treatise intitled,
Woman not inferior to Man, &c.

INTERSPERSED WITH

A Variety of Characters of different Kinds of Women, drawn from the Life.

To which is prefixed

A Dedication to the LADIES.

By a GENTLEMAN.

Fools they muſt have, or elſe they cannot ſway:
For none but Fools will *Womankind* obey.
Some Few with Beauty may ſubdue the Strong;
A mighty Empire! but it laſts not long.
Th'obſequious Lover, when he loweſt lies,
Submits to conquer, and but kneels to riſe. Dryden.

LONDON:

Printed for J. Robinson, at the *Golden-Lion* in *Ludgate-ſtreet*. 1744.

[Price One Shilling.]

A man hits back (1744).

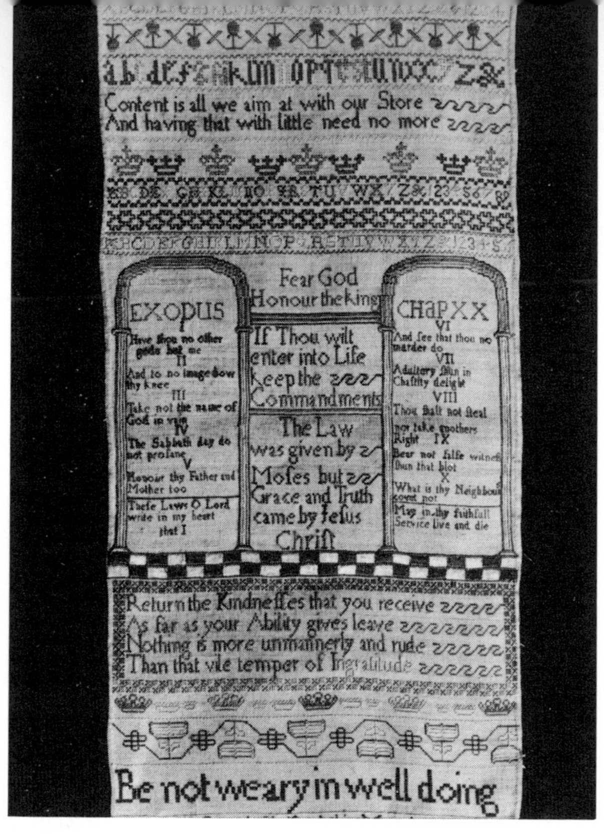

Embroidery and religion taught simultaneously. Sampler worked by a child in silk on linen, about 1730. Stitches used are cross, Algerian eye and satin.

according to the school. On leaving they were given a Bible, a Prayer Book, and 40s. to give them a start towards earning a living (e.g. to pay for an apprenticeship).

Some charity school boys made good use of their education. Perhaps their most famous Old Boy was Warren Hastings (1732-1818), the first governor-general of British India. And some charity schools prospered exceptionally. In Liverpool it was the Grammar School which closed while the Bluecoat charity school founded by Bryan Blundell has survived until today.

Education of girls

Lady Mary Wortley Montagu was not typical of the times. Her learning would have been more appropriate in the Elizabethan Age. But her warning (p. 92) *was* typical: 'Conceal your learning.' Sarah, Duchess of Marlborough, perhaps the most famous Englishwoman of the first half of the eighteenth century, far from knowing Latin and Greek, did not know any foreign language, and despite her prolific use of English never learned to write it grammatically or spell it correctly.

The charity schools were for girls as well as boys, but the girls spent a good deal of their time on practical work such as sewing (see above). There were few female equivalents of the boys' endowed grammar schools. Girls who were not taught at home could go to private day or boarding schools, if their parents were able to pay. Here the accent was on *gentility*. Girls, or rather 'gentlewomen', as the advertisements for schools called them, were to be 'soberly Educated, and taught all sorts of Learning fit for young Gentlewomen'. Reading, writing, a little French, singing, playing the harpsichord or the spinet, painting and dancing were the kind of Learning which was meant—quite a formidable list if they had all been seriously studied; but they seldom were.

Gibbs's Building, King's College, Cambridge.

Members of Cambridge University at the Pot Fair, which was an important annual event in the eighteenth century. The fat don has been tripped by a dog.

Cambridge University

> Now algebra, geometry,
> Arithmetic, astronomy,
> Optics, chronology, and statics,
> All tiresome points of mathematics. . . .

The wider range of studies provided by the universities prompted an undergraduate of King's College, Cambridge, to write the above lines in 1716. Buildings were changing as well as the curriculum. Not many years after the above lines were written, the Aberdonian architect James Gibbs (1682-1754), who had built St. Martin-in-the-Fields and other London churches, designed the Fellows' building, which is now the most conspicuous part of King's College after the chapel. Gibbs also designed the Senate House, in which those who pass their examinations have their degrees conferred upon them. The great library of Trinity College, decorated inside with carvings by Grinling Gibbons, was designed by Wren. No new colleges were founded between 1588 and 1800 but Cambridge was favoured by the Hanoverian kings and prospered during the eighteenth century.

Bentley encourages science

From 1700 to 1740 one of the greatest British classical scholars, Richard Bentley, was master of Trinity. Though a classics man, he gave science its chance. He had an observatory built at Trinity for the first Professor of Astronomy and fitted up a laboratory for the first Professor of Chemistry. Prosperity however did not result in scholarship being generally admired. Trinity, like other colleges, had a hard core of Fellows who were more interested in good living than in learning or teaching. They twice tried to get rid of Bentley, whom they particularly resented, because he himself had been an undergraduate not at Trinity, but at St. John's.

Oxford University

Oxford was Jacobite (it had been Charles I's capital), but one new college, Worcester, was founded (1714) and, as at Cambridge, some of the most prominent and distinguished buildings are from the late seventeenth century and early eighteenth century—the Sheldonian Theatre (Wren, 1669), 'Tom Tower' (Wren, 1682), the Radcliffe Camera (Gibbs, 1749), All Souls College, and Queen's College.

Queen's was largely rebuilt. A new chapel was consecrated and in 1732, to improve discipline and morals in the College, new rules were issued, e.g.

> That he [the Student] will regularly attend the Public Meals in the Hall, as well as the Public Prayers in the College Chapel, and behave himself reverently as in the more immediate presence of that Omniscient and All-powerful Being he comes there to worship.
>
> That he will be punctual in attending not only the Private Lectures of his Tutor at his Chambers but likewise Public Lectures Disputations and other Exercises in the Hall.

...That he may not abuse these valuable advantages of Learning and Knowledge or bring a Reproach upon his Character by an Ill Life and Conversation, he is further to promise

That he will endeavour... to keep as free as possible from all Atheistical, Loose and Vicious sort of Company; to be guided by his Tutor in the Choice of his Companions...

That he will, as much as in him lies, avoid frequenting Taverns and other Places of Resort, especially such as are of Ill Fame and Credit.

The Wesleys were at Oxford in the 1720's. Samuel Johnson went up to Pembroke, Oxford, in 1728 (aged 19). The poet Gray went up to Peterhouse. Cambridge, in 1734, Horace Walpole to King's in 1735 (aged 18). Yet in spite of a sprinkling of new buildings and distinguished men and in spite of regulations about reverent behaviour, punctuality, attendance at lectures and avoidance of vicious company, the eighteenth century is usually regarded as a period in which religious and intellectual life at Oxford and Cambridge lacked vigour. A mid-century letter-writer summed up the position in the sentence:

'Our Universities are asleep and the Church snores.'

The Grand Tour of Europe completed an eighteenth century gentleman's education. These gentlemen are in Rome. The date is about 1750, yet they all carry swords, perhaps because they are in a foreign country.

CHAPTER IV

GOING TO CHURCH

'THE Church snores.' Did it? Certainly the eighteenth century is not a period which historians of the Church of England refer to with pride. 'With the accession of the Hanoverian line', we read, 'the church entered on a period of feeble life and inaction: many church fabrics were neglected; daily services were discontinued; holy days were disregarded; Holy Communion was infrequent; the poor were little cared for; and though the church remained popular, the clergy were lazy and held in contempt.'

Bad Parsons

Two of the nastiest parsons in the fiction of the time are Thwackum (*Tom Jones*) and the chaplain of Newgate (*Moll Flanders*). The latter visited Moll Flanders and tried to make her confess; but 'he said so little to the purpose that I had no manner of consolation from him; and then to observe the poor creature preaching confession and repentance to me in the morning, and find him drunk with brandy by noon, this had something in it so shocking, that I began to nauseate the man...' What she means is: He made me sick.

Tom Jones's tutor, The Reverend Roger Thwackum, who, you will remember, was 'a fellow of a college, with a great reputation for learning religion and sobriety

The Sleeping Congregation by Hogarth (1756). The parson is preaching, in a black gown, with an hour glass at his side. To conduct the service he had a lower position (and wore a surplice). Below sat the clerk. Hence the term 'three-decker pulpit' (p. 119). The clerk has kept awake and is looking at the girl who has fallen asleep with her Prayer Book open at the marriage service.

of manners', was not lazy. He showed no lack of energy in educating Jones, in conducting philosophical discussions with his employer, and in courting his employer's widowed sister. But he lacked an essential Christian quality. He had 'utterly discarded all natural goodness of heart'. He can certainly be reckoned among the clergy who were 'held in contempt'. He was despicable.

A good Parson

Not so Parson Abraham Adams (*Joseph Andrews*), whom we have already met (p. 95) voicing his disapproval of 'public schools'. He too was a scholar. He knew Greek, Latin, French, Italian and Spanish and had written three volumes of sermons, by the sale of which he hoped to restore his family's fortunes. For Adams was a village clergyman with a wife and six children to support on an income of £23 a year. Though fifty years old, he was only the curate, not the rector of the parish. The squire regarded him as a kind of domestic servant; when he called, he was given his mug of ale in the kitchen; but those who knew him well loved him deeply. He was generous, friendly, brave and *simple* in the best sense of the word; that is to say, he assumed that others were as good-hearted as he was. 'As he had never any intention to deceive, so he never suspected such a design in others.'

The Marriage from Hogarth's series of paintings called *A Rake's Progress*. St. Marylebone Church is shown, in a poor state of repair, and two dogs have been allowed in. The bride is a rich widow. The bridegroom is more interested in her maid.

The lantern of this church, which has now been enlarged to become Portsmouth Cathedral, was built to serve partly as a lookout post during Queen Anne's reign.

It is not surprising that Adams failed to find a market for his sermons. In talking about them to a bookseller (who combined selling with publishing, see p. 150) he gave, as an example of their contents, the opinion that 'a virtuous and good Turk, or heathen' was more acceptable in the sight of his Creator than a vicious and wicked Christian. This put the bookseller off immediately. He said he did not think there would be much sale for a book containing such opinions, of which the clergy would certainly disapprove.

'The Vicar of Bray'

Fielding does not explain how Adams managed to get books to read. Living deep in the country, he can hardly have been one of the fortunate few who benefited by a church lending library scheme, begun during Queen

Anne's reign. Through this scheme, by 1711, about forty-five towns in England were receiving collections of religious books intended to keep the clergy up to date with the arguments then being conducted between 'High Churchmen' and 'Low Churchmen', two expressions which had recently come into use. The High Churchman was fiercely against nonconformity and usually a Tory in politics. The Low Churchman was fiercely against Popery and inclined to support the Whigs. Verses 4 and 5 of *The Vicar of Bray*, a song dating from c. 1720, illustrate the difference ('Pudding time' means a time of prosperity, when there is plenty of pudding to eat):

When royal Anne became our Queen,
  The Church of England's glory,
Another face of things was seen,
  And I became a Tory;
Occasional conformists base,
  I blam'd their moderation;
And thought the Church in danger was,
  By such prevarication.

Chorus And this is law I will maintain,
  Until my dying day, Sir,
That whatsoever King shall reign,
  I'll still be the Vicar of Bray, Sir.

When George in pudding-time came o'er,
  And moderate men looked big, Sir,
My principles I chang'd once more,
  And so became a Whig, Sir;
And thus preferment I procur'd
  From our new faith's-defender;
And almost every day abjur'd
  The Pope and the Pretender.

Chorus And this is law, &c.

Poor parsons

The fictitious Adams was no doubt kindlier than any real parson, but many of these may have been kinder

‘Not every clergyman remained poor’.

at the outset of their careers than they were later. A kind heart can be hardened by circumstances. In order to get a position as a rector or curate, a man had to ingratiate himself with the rich and influential person who owned the ‘living’. If he was lucky and got the post, the income was usually small. It might have been higher than Adams’s £24; John Wesley (p. 133) as a young man accepted a curacy of £30 a year and many livings were worth about £50 a year; but it might have been as low as £10. Hence the complaint (p. 109) that the poor were little cared for. Most parsons were poor themselves. They did not even enjoy a high position in the social scale. As we have seen, if they called at a big house, they were more likely to be entertained in the kitchen than the dining room. They were nearer to Chaucer’s Poor Parson than to the middle-class clergy of the nineteenth and twentieth centuries.

Prospects of promotion

The impoverished state of her clergy did not escape the notice of Queen Anne, who loved the Church. Queen Anne's Bounty, a fund set up in 1704, was beginning to alleviate the distress of the poorest clergy by the reign of George II, who would not have been likely to make such provision of his own accord. It has also to be remembered that not every clergyman remained poor. Some obtained the incomes of several livings without looking after them. (This practice, 'pluralism', had been going on for centuries.) Some became fellows of colleges, like Thwackum. This meant that they could not marry. On the other hand if a wealthy enough woman could be found she might be able to keep one as comfortably as King's or Balliol and it would be worth surrendering the fellowship. Thwackum seemed to think so.

Finally you could become a Bishop or a Dean—a person of influence and affluence received in the best society. Because of this, younger sons of the nobility and gentry were beginning to enter the church with their eyes on promotion. But it was also possible for a poor boy to become a great man by entering the church. This possibility, like pluralism, had existed since the Middle Ages.

Even Bishops were not without their troubles. While the bishopric of Durham was worth £6,000 a year and Winchester £5,000, Bristol only brought in £450. There were also complaints about the physical strain of confirmation, candidates for which offered themselves in their thousands. In 1737 a bishop gave the figure of 8,922 candidates confirmed in two Yorkshire towns in a few days. He said he was in church from about 9.0 a.m. till 7.0 p.m.

Church Building

You cannot judge the religious fervour of a period in English history by the number or the beauty of the churches built. The later Tudors (Edward VI, Mary and Elizabeth), in whose time men suffered agonies for their faiths, left us the Prayer Book and the first widely read translations of the Bible, but did not build churches. The fiercely devout Cromwellians were not long enough in power to undertake much church building and anyway were little inclined towards glorifying God in this way. It was the fire of London, not the fire of faith, which

St. Martin-in-the-Fields, designed by James Gibbs and consecrated in 1726.

gave us St. Paul's and Wren's city churches; and their beauty is due to the inspiration of the Renaissance, i.e. the revived interest in the pre-Christian eras of Greece and Rome, not to any religious revival. In the eighteenth century wealth and population increased, so churches were built in newly developed areas—fifty in London, begun in Queen Anne's reign, and others throughout the country, e.g. St. Anne's, Manchester, St. Philip's, Birmingham, All Saints', Derby (now Derby Cathedral), St. Nicholas's, Nottingham.

Inside the church

Because the taste of the time was good, the churches were beautiful. Stained glass and interior decoration, however, were considered Popish. You will not find much eighteenth century stained glass, though there is some in Westminster Abbey. Wren had intended that Italian artists should decorate the inside of the dome of St. Paul's with mosaic; but he was overruled.

Although the outside of eighteenth century churches is often splendid, they have a feature inside—the gallery—which they owe to Puritan simplicity. Puritan places of worship were small and a gallery enabled a bigger congregation to be squeezed in. Anglican churches adopted the idea. Galleries were built into existing churches and became a usual feature of new ones built in the eighteenth century. Thus the age which is remembered for its lack of religious fervour is the one whose churches can be recognized by this device for crowding people in. It is only fair to add, however, that the gallery was also an economy, since it enabled the architect to confine himself to a smaller site.

These galleries are easy to find in London, e.g. at St. George's, Hanover Square (1724), at St. Martin-in-the-Fields (1726) or at St. James's, Piccadilly (completed in 1684 and recently rebuilt after bombing in 1940);

but the three-decker pulpits which were characteristic of the period have disappeared. The parish clerk sat on the lowest level. The parson conducted the service from the level immediately above and mounted to the top to preach his sermon. Sometimes there was a two-decker desk for clerk and parson, with a separate pulpit.

In the Middle Ages people had stood in church. Seats began to appear in Elizabethan times. By the eighteenth century there was seating for all according to their station, from charity school-children on benches just below the pulpit, to the gentry in box pews as big as small rooms, where a fire could be lit; here, during the interminable sermon, it was possible to smoke a pipe, have something to eat or take a nap.

In a sense, therefore, it may sometimes have been partially true that 'the Church snored', but not the church attended by Joseph Addison's genial character, Sir Roger de Coverley, of whom we hear that:

> As Sir Roger is Landlord to the whole Congregation, he keeps them in very good Order, and will suffer no Body to sleep in it besides himself; for if by chance he has been surprized into a short Nap at Sermon, upon recovering out of it he stands up and looks about him, and if he sees any Body else nodding, either wakes them himself, or sends his Servant to them... As soon as the Sermon is finished, no Body presumes to stir till Sir Roger is gone out of the Church. The Knight walks down from his Seat in the Chancel between a Double Row of his Tenants, that stand bowing to him, on each Side; and every now and then enquires how such an one's Wife, or Mother, or Son, or Father do, whom he does not see at Church; which is understood as a secret reprimand to the Person that is absent.

As daily services fell into disuse, most churches stood quiet during the week, but the practice of using cathedrals as places for a stroll and a chat still persisted. The tradition had grown up in old St. Paul's and was continued in the new building. At Durham and Norwich

t. Clement Danes, built by Wren, bombed in World War II and :ored by the Royal Air Force, is reconsecrated in the presence of een Elizabeth II (1958).

the use of the nave as a short cut for people on foot was only stopped in the middle of the century. In contrast, two hundred years later, the architect of the new Coventry cathedral took special pains to encourage people to pass almost through the cathedral. A paved path leads through the porch beside the west door, so that passers-by can have the pleasure of looking into the cathedral, even if they do not worship there.

Hymns

The church may have snored, but it also sang. For the first time during this undevout century hymns as well as the traditional psalms began to be heard, accompanied on the organ in town and by various musicians in country churches.

In a list of original British hymns published a hundred years ago 1,410 authors are named. Of these 1,213 wrote their hymns later than 1707, the year of Fielding's birth. In hymn-books used today a substantial proportion of the hymns, though not so many of the tunes, are from the eighteenth century. It would be interesting to make a count of hymns according to date in whatever hymn-book you use and see which period of fifty years has contributed the greatest number. The late eighteenth century and the nineteenth century are likely to come out on top, but some very well known hymns were written in Fielding's lifetime.

Joseph Addison (1672-1719) was the son of a successful clergyman, who became a dean. He gained a fellowship at Magdalen College, Oxford, and intended to enter the church himself; instead he studied law and went into politics, without achieving any great success. It was as an essayist that he became famous. His writing, which appeared chiefly in the *Spectator,* was satirical, though not bitterly so, and in the course of his attacks on the low morals and irreligion of the time he wrote three

Joseph Addison. He has recently broken the seal and opened a letter (*left*). Note how it is folded. There were no envelopes.

hymns. They appeared at the close of essays in the *Spectator* during the late summer of 1712 and their first lines, still familiar to many, are:

'How are thy servants blest'
'When all thy mercies, O my God'
'The spacious firmament on high'

At midnight on Midsummer Day 1719 Joseph Addison was buried in Westminster Abbey. Scholars of Westminster School stood round the open grave holding tapers. One of them, Charles Wesley, aged eleven, lived to the age of eighty-one. During his extremely active life, of which more will be said later (p. 132), he wrote over 6,500 hymns. Some of the most famous are:

'Hark! the herald angels sing'
'Love divine, all love excelling'
'Christ, whose glory fills the skies'
'Jesu, Lover of my soul'
'O, for a thousand tongues to sing'
'Christ the Lord is risen to-day'
'Soldiers of Christ arise'

Among Charles Wesley's admirers was Isaac Watts (1674-1748), a nonconformist minister. He too has made a considerable contribution to the hymnals of today. Among his six hundred compositions are:

'Jesus shall reign where'er the sun'
'Oh God, our help in ages past'
'When I survey the wondrous Cross'
'There is a land of pure delight'

Why did Watts write hymns? He felt that the Psalms of David no longer inspired people. In the Preface of his book of *Hymns and Spiritual Songs* (1720) he wrote:

> To see the dull indifference, the negligent, and the thoughtless air, that sits upon the faces of a whole assembly, while the psalm is on their lips, might tempt even a charitable observer to suspect the fervency of inward religion; and it is much to be feared, that the minds of most of the worshippers are absent or unconcerned.

What was wrong with the Psalms? Watts does not complain of the tunes, but of the content. Some of them, he says, are contrary to the spirit of the gospel (i.e. of the New Testament) and to the new commandment 'love your enemies':

> When we are just entering into an evangelical frame of mind... the very next line perhaps which the clerk parcels out unto us, hath something in it so extremely Jewish and cloudy, that darkens our sight of God the Saviour.

(Note the reference to the practice of singing line by line, following the parish clerk who led the singing from his seat below the pulpit.)

Watts does not suggest that all Psalm singing should stop; he admires the Psalter:

> Nothing can be supposed more proper to raise a pious soul to heaven, than some parts of that book . . . but it must be acknowledged still, that there are a thousand lines in it which were not made for a church in our days.

So to supply the deficiencies of the Psalter, Watts wrote his hymns. They are gentler than Charles Wesley's, which, it has been said, were 'forged and sung in the furnace of persecution'. The reputation of the two as writers is equally high, in spite of Watts's much smaller output. But there was one hymn of Charles Wesley's of which Watts said that he would rather have written it than any of his own. It is not one of the best known. It is called 'Wrestling Jacob' and was written in 1742. Here is the first verse:

> Come, O Thou Traveller unknown,
> Whom still I hold, but cannot see,
> My company before is gone
> And I am left alone with Thee.
> With Thee all night I mean to stay,
> And wrestle till the break of day.

Another nonconformist minister, Dr. Philip Doddridge (1702–1751), wrote hymns connected with his sermons. A sermon preached on Luke 12, 35-38, which includes the words: 'Blessed are those servants, whom the Lord when he cometh shall find watching' was followed by the hymn: 'Ye servants of the Lord'. A sermon on the vow which Jacob made at Bethel (Genesis 28, 20-22) was followed by the hymn 'O God of Bethel [or 'of Jacob'] by whose hand'.

A new hymn matching the sermon is all very well, but how do you learn the words and the tune? Doddridge sang the hymns line by line and the congregation sang each line after him. Even if he could have afforded to have every hymn printed, not all the congregation would have been able to read them. Books of hymns were published and members of the congregation who could both afford them and read them were no doubt a great help. But in most neighbourhoods, particularly in the country, such people must have been in a minority. Sir Roger de Coverley engaged a singing master, as we learn in the course of the following description:

> My Friend Sir Roger being a good Churchman, has beautified the Inside of his Church with several texts of his own chusing; he has likewise given a handsome Pulpit Cloth, and railed in the Communion Table at his own expence. He has often told me, that at his coming to his Estate he found his Parishioners very irregular; and that in order to make them kneel and join in the Responses he gave every one of them a Hassock and a Common Prayer Book: and at the same time employed an itinerant Singing Master, who goes about the Country for that Purpose, to instruct them rightly in the Tunes of the Psalms; upon which they now very much value themselves, and indeed out-do most of the Country Churches that I have ever heard.

Some of the hymn-books published included a collection of new tunes, but the hymn-writers mentioned above were not musicians and their hymns were at first sung to various traditional tunes. It was not till the nineteenth century that 'Hark! the herald angels sing' acquired the tune to which it is now sung. The German composer Mendelssohn wrote it. 'Jesu, lover of my soul' is now sung to a tune written in 1861. Eighteenth century tunes have not stood the test of time as well as eighteenth century hymns. At Easter, however, 'Christ the Lord is risen today' is still often sung to a tune first published in 1707 (the author's name is not known); and at Christmas we still sing 'Christians awake' to a tune written about 1750 by John Wainwright, an organist of Stockport in Lancashire, who would not be very pleased if he knew that, owing to a mistake made long after his death, the tune is now known as 'Yorkshire'.

Finally, some advice from Charles Wesley on how to sing hymns:

Sing *lustily* and with good courage. Beware of singing as if you were half dead or half asleep.

Sing *modestly*. Do not bawl, so as to be heard above or distinct from the rest of the congregation.

Sing *in Time* and take care not to sing too slow.

Above all sing *spiritually*. Have an eye to God in every word you sing. Aim at pleasing *Him* more than yourself, or any other creature; so shall your singing be such as the Lord will approve of here, and reward you when He cometh in the clouds of heaven.

Bells

Hymns and psalms were sung by all denominations except Quakers. Bell-ringing was usual only in the Church of England. It is worth finding out the dates of the bells in any church you may visit. A large number are likely to date only from the nineteenth century.

Manuals of the organ on which Handel used to play in the Chapel of the Foundling Hospital. The notes usually white are black, and *vice versa*.

Many were melted down at the dissolution of the monasteries and in the Civil War.

In the eighteenth century, when a church had five bells, four were often sold by the churchwardens to pay bills (e.g. for repairs, which, however, were seldom thorough—whitewashing was used to conceal defects). Change-ringing, an art which had grown up in the seventeenth century, now became less respectable. When a new bell was installed, instead of a pious ceremony, there was an orgy, the bell being temporarily fixed bottom up, so that it could be filled with drink. This at least shows that new bells were being cast and it is known that a Gloucester bell foundry produced about forty a year.

The most famous eighteenth century bell is the Great Bell of St. Paul's (1716). It still hangs in the south tower and serves as the hour bell of the clock. It is called Great Tom and has occasionally been broadcast instead of Big Ben.

Refixing at St. Clement Danes the only bell to survive the bombing of 1941. Its name 'Sanctus', is scratched on the inside.

St. Clement Danes at the beginning of the eighteenth century before the steeple was added.

Services

But how often did the bells ring to summon people to church? Daily services were exceptional by 1750, though a number of London churches still held them. On Sundays, if the clergyman had only one church to look after, he held two services, at one of which he preached a sermon. More than half the London churches had two Sunday services, but the proportion was lower in the country. Surprisingly, in view of the lukewarm attitude to religion which is often noted as a characteristic of these times, the services with sermons were the more popular. Church attendance by everyone at some place of worship was usual. According to the law, attendance was still compulsory. This law was not repealed until Victoria's reign, but it was not strictly enforced. All nonconformists or 'dissenters', except Unitarians, were entitled by the Act of Toleration (1689) to

THE
BOOK
OF
COMMON PRAYER,
And Adminiſtration of the
SACRAMENTS,
AND OTHER
Rites and Ceremonies
OF THE
CHURCH,
According to the Uſe of the
Church of England:
Together with the
PSALTER or PSALMS
OF
DAVID,
Pointed as they are to be Sung or Said in CHURCHES.

OXFORD:
Printed by JOHN BASKETT, Printer to the UNIVERSITY.
M DCC XXXIX.
1739

Title page of Prayer Book (1739).

hold their own services (e.g. Presbyterian, Quaker, Baptist or Congregationalist). In fact, both Unitarians and Catholics usually worshipped undisturbed.

At Church of England services the Prayer Book of 1662 was used. It was not very different from the Church of England Prayer Book of today. The parson wore a cassock with a surplice over it, except during the sermon, when he exchanged the surplice for the black gown which he wore out of doors. (As wigs were now worn, the surplice had to open down the front instead of being slipped on over the head.) The cross was still thought to be Popish. Few were to be seen in churches. Seldom now was a sinner paraded in a white sheet before the congregation; but this medieval practice had not quite died out in some country districts. In the Isle of Man penance was done in a white sheet in church until the nineteenth century.

Communion services were less frequent than today. People of High Church views favoured a weekly celebration but it was more usual to have Communion once a month in towns and between three and seven times a year in the country.

Sunday

Though the number of services decreased, Sunday was still a solemn day. Cromwell's ban on public amusements of any kind still operated. There were no concerts or games, and theatres were closed. Card-playing was forbidden. However, a French visitor gave it as his opinion that the restriction only applied to the middle and lower classes, adding 'Persons of rank, I believe, do not scruple to play. Unfortunately a great number of the people divert themselves in the taverns and these indulge in debauch.' A German visitor complained that on Sunday there were hardly any boats or hackney coaches for hire and that at his inn the landlady would not even allow guests to play the viola da gamba (p. 202) or the flute.

Toleration

Compared with England today, England at the beginning of the eighteenth century may appear to have been intolerant in matters of religion. No one who was not a member of the Church of England could study at Oxford or Cambridge (the only two universities), hold public office or become a member of parliament. But compared with the two previous centuries, during which men had been burned, hanged, imprisoned and persecuted for their beliefs, the eighteenth was tolerant.

Catholics

As we have seen (p. 128) Catholic worship, though against the law, was not usually interfered with, though some arrests were made after the 'fifteen' and 'forty-five' rebellions. There were no public Roman Catholic churches, but throughout England Catholic gentlemen of means kept priests and arranged for worship in their private chapels. Nor were all Catholics dependent on a rich patron. There was already a considerable Catholic group in Liverpool. They had built their own chapel and on Palm Sunday, 1727, 256 palms were distributed. A mob burned the chapel in 1746, but a new meeting place was immediately found.

Occasionally Catholics in a particular district seem to have had the upper hand. In 1706 an Essex priest complained that there were 30 or 40 Papists in his parish under the patronage of Lord Petre. One of them, a farmer:

> is a very impident fellow, giving ill language when I demand what is my due and calls me names and 'twas he or one of his sons I am confident that wrote upon the church wall 'He that preacheth here is a rougue and a dog'.

Quakers

Though enjoying, since the Toleration Act, the same freedom of worship as other nonconformists, Quakers remained unpopular. They were devout and sincere; some of them were beginning to make a name for themselves in commerce, industry and science; but they looked and sounded different from other people. They dressed in simple clothes; the women wore pointed hats; the men refused to wear wigs. They used the second person singular—'thou' and 'thee'—a form which had for centuries been employed only in addressing inferiors or God—and called each other 'brother' or 'sister'. Added to these peculiarities was the shaking or 'quaking' which sometimes overcame these people when inspired to speak at one of their meetings for worship, during much of which all sat in silence.

Business meeting of Quakers. They are simply dressed and wear no wigs. Tom Jones's 'great chair made of rushes' (p. 69) may have looked like the one on the left.

The Quakers were too upright, odd and mysterious for the average man, who often regarded them with suspicion and contempt. They had what we would now call 'advanced' ideas. John Bellers, for instance, in 1714 published proposals for state aid to medicine and medical research. He suggested that severe penalties should be imposed for bribery at elections, which was then general; and he was one of the first to propose the abolition of capital punishment.

Quakers did not confine themselves to brief inspired utterances during their meetings. They produced impressive preachers. One of these, Samuel Bownas, was a countryman and spoke slowly. When he was one day interrupted while preaching he said to the offender: 'Have patience, woman, 'twill be better by an by!' This may have been true of that particular sermon but Quakers in the eighteenth century lacked some of the fire of the seventeenth century in which their movement had been founded. This was also true of the Baptists.

Some Quakers fell asleep during meetings. Furthermore 'Friends' as they are also called, began to think of themselves as a separate, peculiar people, cut off from the ways of the world. 'Marrying out', i.e. marrying a non-Quaker, meant ceasing to be accepted as a Quaker. Thus many young men and women left the movement.

The Wesleys

During his pursuit of Sophia in London, Fielding's Tom Jones became involved with the rich and not altogether respectable Lady Bellaston. Suddenly they were seriously inconvenienced by the landlady of the house where they regularly met. This person 'was now become a methodist, and had that very morning waited upon her ladyship, and after rebuking her very severely for her past life, had positively declared that she would, on no account, be instrumental in carrying on any of her affairs for the future.'

Who were the Methodists and what was their method?

One night in February 1709 a fire raged in the village of Epworth, which stands on a low hill among the flat fields of Lincolnshire. The fire could be seen for miles around, lighting up the tower of the church. The house which was burning was not far from the church; it was, in fact, the rectory, home of the Reverend Samuel Wesley ('Wessley', not 'Wezley' is the usual pronunciation).

In Epworth not many tears were shed over the disaster. The Rev. Samuel, a High Churchman, was unpopular in an area of strong nonconformist traditions. (Many of the Puritans who sailed to America in the *Mayflower* had originally slipped out of England down the Humber, Lincolnshire's northern border.) Furthermore Samuel Wesley was hard up and owed money to some of his

John Wesley.

parishioners. Some say that the rector's enemies in the village caused the fire. Anyway, no lives were lost. The flames died down. But the blaze was symbolic. It was as if sparks that flew upward from Epworth set England on fire. Fire can warm, illumine, agonize and destroy; but it cannot be ignored.

At the time of the fire Samuel Wesley had his wife, three sons and six daughters to support on £50 p.a. These were the survivors of seventeen children whom his wife Susannah, one of a family of two dozen, had born him. His debts are understandable. Nevertheless he had managed to send his eldest son, also called Samuel, to Westminster School in London and this had been worth while, since the boy had now become a King's Scholar and did not have to be paid for. The second son, John, aged five, was still at home, subjected with his sisters to the stern educational system devised by his mother (p. 89). Charles was a baby. Later both boys went, like their elder brother, to school in London. John went to Charterhouse on a scholarship at the age of eleven. Charles went to Westminster when he was eight and

John Wesley's tomb, behind the Chapel in City Road, London.

became a King's Scholar. When they grew up, they remained short in stature, like their father, who was only five foot tall.

Of the three Wesley sons, only Sam remained content with a normal career. From Westminster he went up to Christ Church, Oxford, returned to teach at his old school, became a parson and in 1732 was made headmaster of Blundell's School in Devon. He became known as a scholar and a poet and died in 1739, just as his brothers and their 'method' were becoming known.

Methodism

This 'method' consisted in a rigorously strict way of life, which John and Charles Wesley, together with a group of about twenty-five friends, including George Whitefield, adopted at Oxford. They met daily to read the Bible and other serious works and to talk frankly about how they ought to live. They fasted twice a week and went to Communion every Sunday (a practice very uncommon at the time, see p. 129). They rose very early (John Wesley started his day at 4.0 a.m.), lay out of doors in winter frosts, looked after the sick and spent time visiting prisoners in the gaol, a place which no one else approached unless they had to. The group called themselves the Holy Club, but others referred to them contemptuously as 'methodists' and John Wesley later adopted this as the official name of his movement.

John and Charles were both ordained as Church of England clergymen like their father and in 1735 they went to the colony of Georgia on the staff of the governor, hoping to serve the community and to do missionary work among the Indians. Unfortunately they managed to make themselves thoroughly unpopular. John fell in love, caused acute unhappiness to the girl and himself, and then did not marry. By 1738 both brothers were back in England.

It was in the summer of that year that they experienced a kind of conversion, which led them to dedicate their lives to fervent Christian leadership. John has described how he was at a meeting in Aldersgate, London. A passage from Luther was being read. Then, he writes:

> I felt my heart strangely warmed. I felt I did trust in Christ, Christ alone, for salvation.

The Wesleys were devoted to the Church of England and it was only because of the opposition of local clergy that meetings came to be held wherever a room could be provided, or in the open air. John Wesley did not leave the Church of England until 1784; Charles never did, which explains why he was buried in the churchyard of St. Marylebone Parish Church, while his brother lies in the graveyard of City Road chapel.

Charles's 6,500 hymns have already been mentioned (p. 121). As well as writing hymns he travelled and preached, but he also achieved a settled married life, which his brother never did. John married late. His wife bore him no children and finally left him. She was not prepared to travel the country on horseback in all weathers meeting Methodist groups and listening to her husband's sermons. In the fifty-three years left to him after the beginning of his mission in 1738 he kept a journal and wrote many letters. It has thus been possible to calculate that he travelled about a quarter of a million miles and preached over forty thousand sermons, an average of fifteen a week. But most of this activity belongs to the period after 1750. It was

Inside Bevis Marks Synagogue, which has a gallery, like churches and chapels built at the same time.

then that Methodism and the Industrial Revolution expanded side by side. Methodists were well equipped to endure the miseries of the factory system but they were never encouraged to fight it.

Finally, it should be said that Methodists hated as fiercely as they loved. They were no friends of the Roman Catholics, nor of the Jews.

Jews

A chapter on going to church may perhaps be allowed a concluding paragraph on going to the synagogue. After being excluded from England by Edward III, Jews, with a few exceptions, had not been allowed in again until the time of Cromwell. First came Spanish and Portuguese Jews, mostly well off. They were allowed freedom of worship and engaged a Quaker to build the synagogue which still stands in Bevis Marks in the City of London. (It is said that the Quaker did the work at cost price, out of piety.) Jews from central and eastern Europe, often poor and often fugitives from persecution, began to immigrate at the end of the seventeenth century. Their synagogue, known as the Great Synagogue, near Aldgate, opened in 1722. It was bombed in World War II and has been rebuilt.

Jews were not allowed to be naturalized and in 1753, when there were about 5,000 Jews in England, an Act making their naturalization legal had to be repealed immediately owing to the violent anti-Semitism of the London mob. A further disadvantage for Jews was that they might not be apprenticed to a Christian master. As a result they were virtually excluded from learning a skilled trade. Many were driven to becoming pedlars or criminals.

This brings us to the subject of the next chapter. How did the more fortunate majority of Englishmen, and sometimes Englishwomen, earn their living?

CHAPTER V

EARNING A LIVING

TOM JONES had money worries, but it cannot be said that earning a living was a problem either for him or for many of the people with whom he was closely associated. Mr. Allworthy, Jones's foster-father, owed his name to the fact that he was *worthy* and had, nearly, *all*—'an agreeable person, a sound constitution, a solid understanding, a benevolent heart and one of the largest estates in the country.' Mr. Western, the neighbouring landowner and father of the exquisite Sophia, was also a man of ample means. But there are plenty of minor characters who provide examples of ways in which one might try to earn a living in Tom Jones's England.

A schoolmaster

Mr. Partridge, a schoolmaster, was 'one of the best-natured fellows in the world', witty, and very popular among the local gentry. He spent more time in their houses than in his school (9 pupils). As to his salary, 'it would hardly have indulged the schoolmaster in the luxuries of life, had he not added to this office those of clerk and barber, and had not Mr. Allworthy added to the whole an annuity of ten pounds, which the poor man received every Christmas... Among his other treasures, the pedagogue had a wife, whom he married out of Mr. Allworthy's kitchen for her fortune, viz. twenty pounds, which she had there amassed.'

Mr Porter please to pay Richd Drayton forty Shillings for half A Years Salary Due at Lady Day Last Being Master of the Singing School

Sept: 20:
1748 E Freeman Mayor

Recd of Mr Geo: Porter the full Content of this Note p RD Drayton

The Mayor of Coventry authorizes payment of forty shillings for a half year's work to the Master of the Singing School, who acknowledges receipt.

A chandler

'Chandler' originally meant a seller of candles, but the chandler's shop was now a grocery or, in a village, a general store. For women the chandler's was 'the known seat of all the news; or, as it is vulgarly called, gossiping, in every parish in England.'

Medical men

Dr. Y and Dr. Z who arrived after their patient had died, 'were at a loss how to apply that portion of time which it is usual and decent to remain for their fee' and therefore spent it in arguing about whether the patient had died of apoplexy (Dr. Y's view) or of epilepsy (the firm conviction of Dr. Z).

When Tom had broken his arm while saving Sophia from a hunting accident, Squire Western shouted cheerfully 'We will get a joiner to mend it again'; however, a surgeon was found. He first insisted on 'bleeding'

Sophia, i.e. taking blood from her arm. This was thought to alleviate nervousness or fever. He then dealt with Jones, whom he ordered to be stripped to his shirt. Then he began to stretch and examine the arm 'in such a manner that the tortures he put him to caused Jones to make several wry faces; which the surgeon observing, greatly wondered at, crying 'What is the matter, sir? I am sure it is impossible I should hurt you.'

Such was the faith in bleeding as a remedy that on another occasion, when Jones had been hit on the head with a bottle and was lying in a pool of blood, everyone nevertheless shouted: 'Bleed him', and when Jones was later recovering in bed the surgeon still wanted to bleed him. 'Will you be blooded or no?' he cried in a rage, and when Jones refused, 'Then I wash my hands of you and I desire you to pay me for the trouble I have had already. Two journeys at 5s., two dressings at 5s.' But he did not get his money.

However, not all Fielding's doctors and surgeons are horrible. He describes one surgeon who acted like a good Samaritan, dressing his patient's wounds, taking him to an inn and offering to lend him money. As we shall see in Chapter VIII, he had to call upon medical men himself a good deal and often speaks well of them.

'Dr.' or 'Mr.'?

Fielding is not precise in his use of the title 'Dr.'. He will write 'Dr.' before a man's name in one sentence and 'Mr.' in another and will talk of him either as 'the doctor' or as 'the surgeon'. More often than not the title Dr. was undeserved. Real doctors—men who had taken a degree in medicine at Cambridge or Oxford, in Scotland, or abroad—were rare in country districts, where there would usually have been only an apothecary for medicines and a surgeon for dressing wounds and for amputations. Surgeons, until 1745, were licensed by the Barber–Surgeons' Company and, although they were in a separate section of the Company from the members whose business was shaving, hairdressing and the care of wigs, they were considered inferior to physicians, who either had a university degree or were licensed by the College of Physicians in London or by the bishop of the diocese where they lived.

In 1745 the Surgeons separated entirely from the Barbers, but what contributed most to the raising of their status was the instruction provided by John Hunter, beginning in 1748. His students had to dissect bodies themselves instead of being taught largely by diagrams. His best remembered sentence occurs in one of his letters: 'Why think, why not try an experiment?'

However, throughout our period and for some time afterwards the order of importance amongst medical people was:

Physicians
Surgeons
Apothecaries

Apothecaries mixed and sold drugs. There were no dentists. Surgeons and others drew teeth. In France,

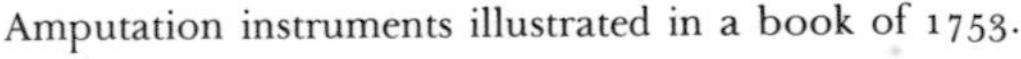
Amputation instruments illustrated in a book of 1753.

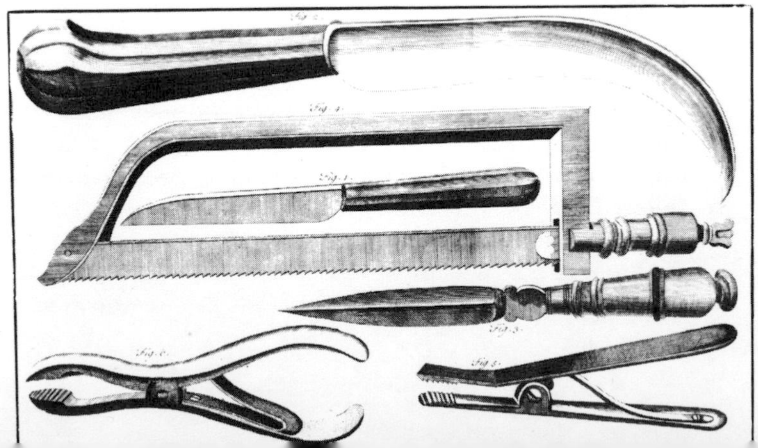

however, you could have artificial teeth to fill gaps and a defective tooth could be fitted with a gold crown.

Physicians

It was possible to start as an apothecary and rise higher. Dr. John Fothergill (1712-1780), a Quaker, was apprenticed to an apothecary at the age of sixteen and took the degree of doctor of medicine in Edinburgh (as a nonconformist he was excluded from Cambridge and Oxford).

The Edinburgh medical school was beginning to be famous; but the best medical education in Europe was at this time provided by a tall, modest Dutchman called Hermann Boerhaave (1668-1738), at the University of Leyden.

When Fothergill set up in practice as a physician, he prescribed simple drugs and emphasized the importance of a wholesome diet, cleanliness and fresh air. But many doctors still had faith in extraordinary traditional remedies of which the following are a few sample ingredients: Wind pipes of sheep cleansed and dried in an oven, frogs' livers, toads burned to ashes and ground to powder, goose dung gathered in springtime, ravens' flesh, crabs' claws, elks' hoofs and live hog lice.

Thermometer, stethoscope and feeling the pulse

If you are ill nowadays and call a doctor, the first thing he will probably do will be to take your temperature; he will then feel your pulse; he may next take out his stethoscope and listen to your chest. A doctor in the first half of the eighteenth century had no thermometer and no stethoscope. He felt the pulse of his patient, but could not time it accurately, because he had not a watch with a second-hand.

Thermometers for measuring air temperature were

improved by Fahrenheit, Celsius and Réaumur in the first half of the century, but though certain doctors experimented with clinical thermometers (e.g. John Hunter took the temperatures of animals), temperature-taking did not become a regular medical routine until halfway through the nineteenth century. The stethoscope too was a nineteenth century invention. Accurate pulse measurement was assisted by a Lichfield doctor, Sir John Floyer (1649-1734), who introduced a watch which ran for exactly one minute (but he also sent the child Samuel Johnson to London to be touched by Queen Anne for 'King's Evil' or scrofula, a disease affecting the glands, which she was the last monarch to try and cure by royal magic).

Forceps used by Smellie at the birth of babies. Midwives and patients distrusted the new instrument, so Smellie bound it with leather to stop any clinking noise and thus prevent anyone knowing what he was doing.

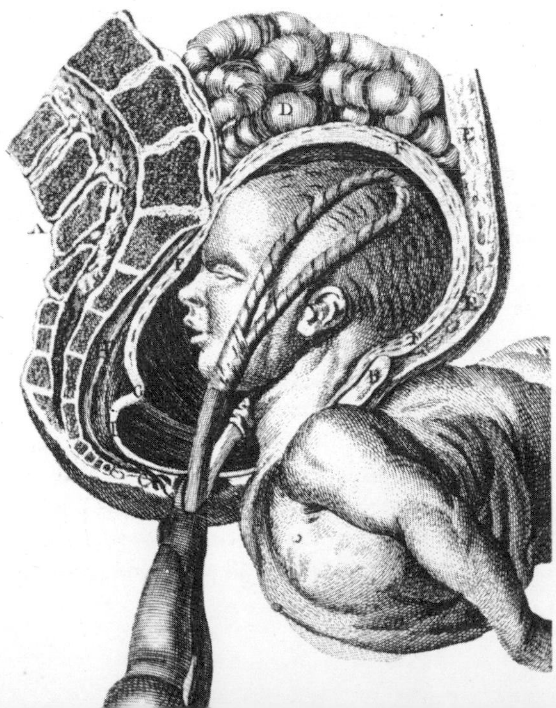

Childbirth

Women could not become doctors, though Fielding mentions a woman who drew teeth (p. 241) and there were some successful female quacks (e.g. Joanna Stevens, who made thousands of pounds out of some medicines, one of which consisted largely of soap: it was calculated that Sir Robert Walpole swallowed 180 pounds of soap while he was one of her patients).

During childbirth, however, midwives were in charge and most women would not have dreamed of calling a doctor. Doctors were not well trained in midwifery until Dr. William Smellie (1697–1763) came from Scotland to London about 1740. His courses included demonstration of the use of forceps in childbirth. Obstetrical (child-birth) forceps had been invented a century before by a Dr. Chamberlen; but contrary to what has since become the medical code of honour, he and his family kept the invention secret. Only when the last of his descendants died without an heir in 1728 did the forceps become generally known.

Smellie was joined in London by William Hunter (1718–1783) who founded the Windmill Street School of Anatomy and became a famous obstetrician. Do not confuse him with his still more famous younger brother, John (p. 141).

Inoculation

A woman who was neither quack nor midwife, but who greatly influenced the medical profession at this time, was Lady Mary Wortley Montagu. Her husband was a diplomat and while living with him in Constantinople she learned about inoculation against small-pox, which was practised there. In 1721 she persuaded George II to take an interest. By his orders experiments were carried out on convicts, and when these proved successful wealthy people began to have themselves and their children inoculated. But the first free inoculations were not introduced until the middle of the century and even after that the movement spread very slowly, in spite of the large number of deaths or disfigurements from small-pox. The disease was not conquered until after Jenner's discovery of vaccination towards the end of the century.

Navy and army doctors

The best-known eighteenth century ships' surgeon is Tobias Smollett (1721-1771). But Smollett is famous for his novels (e.g. *Roderick Random* and *The Adventures of Peregrine Pickle*), not for his surgery. James Lind (1716-1794) was a doctor who stayed a doctor. He entered the navy at the age of twenty-three and served for nine years, mostly on long voyages to the tropics. It was nearly two hundred years since Richard Hawkins had given oranges and lemons to his men in order to combat scurvy, but Lind was shocked to find that this horrible disease was still rampant on long voyages. Hawkins's example had not been followed. The seaman's diet ('putrid beef, rancid pork, mouldy biscuit and bad water') still lacked the essential fresh fruit or green vegetables. Lord Anson, on his voyage round the world (1740-1744), lost three-quarters of his men through scurvy.

Lind's book *A treatise of the scurvy* (1753) made suggestions for preventing the disease, in particular by drinking lemon juice. It took the navy nearly half a century to adopt Lind's proposals, but in 1795 the issue of lemon juice in His Majesty's ships was made compulsory and scurvy almost disappeared within a year. Later, limes were used, so Americans call British sailors 'Limeys'.

Meanwhile the army too had a remarkable doctor—Sir John Pringle (1707-1782), who had studied at St.

Andrews, Edinburgh and Leyden. At the battle of Dettingen (1743) he arranged with the French commander for the military hospitals of both sides to be free from attack, thus laying the foundation on which Henri Dunant built, when he founded the Red Cross a hundred and twenty years later.

A year before Lind published his book on scurvy, Pringle's *Observations on the diseases of the Army* appeared (1752) and led to improvements in, for instance, barracks and military hospitals.

A mixed bunch

We have come a long way from the rough country doctors who crossed Tom Jones's path. This does not mean that the medical men invented by Fielding are simply caricatures. The real ones whom he describes in *A voyage to Lisbon* (Chapter VIII) are a very mixed bunch too. The truth is that medicine attracted geniuses, idealists, incompetents, go-getters, cheats and average citizens. I wish I could give them more space.

Farmers

Statements about farming, like statements about medicine, during the first half of the eighteenth century, depend on your point of view. To us, looking back, the names of Jethro Tull (1674-1741) and Lord Townshend (1674-1738) bulk large. The former introduced seed

From *The Times* of 26 August, 1963.

Science and Medicine:

Battle Against Smallpox Not Yet Wo

From Our Medical Correspondent

The control of disease has proved so successful in recent years that the public has been lulled into a false sense of security. Our relative freedom from the old scourges of mankind, such as tuberculosis, smallpox and typhoid fever, is being taken for granted, and the vital point is being overlooked that this freedom is only achieved by continued vigilance. The battle is not won—indeed, it probably never will be. All that we have is an unstable truce.

drilling and horse hoeing, the latter four-fold crop rotation (wheat, turnips, barley, clover) and the large-scale cultivation of turnips as fodder. But these developments were unknown to most farmers at the time. Whether they were gentlemen or peasants their methods were usually wasteful and unscientific. The medieval open-field strip system was still widely used.

Inefficient or not, some farmers made a lot of money and would not have been surprised had they known that their lifetime would later be regarded by some as the golden age of English agriculture. But about half the country's population worked at some sort of farming, including the raising of sheep and cattle, and the age was only golden for a minority of these. In the country as in the towns acute and widespread poverty was a constant problem.

Threepence a day

Though at times during her life she associated with the wealthy, Moll Flanders knew what poverty meant.

'What can you earn?' she was asked, at the age of eight. 'What can you get a day at your work?'

'Threepence', said I, 'when I spin, and fourpence when I work plain work [i.e. sewing].' She was a tiny part of the great woollen industry, which was more important than any other, except agriculture, in providing employment and making merchants rich (see *The Elizabethan Age*). Defoe, in his *Tour*, wrote an enthusiastic description of cloth-workers in the West Riding of Yorkshire, who were now beginning to outstrip their rivals of East Anglia and the West of England. Kay's flying shuttle, invented in 1733 helped them to increase their lead still further, because it was less useful on the narrow East Anglian looms than on the broadcloth looms of Yorkshire.

Shopping in the Strand in 1740, by which time glass windows for shops had become usual.

A gentleman draper

A draper (a dealer in cloth) was one of several husbands to whom Moll was married at different times. She does not tell us anything about how he conducted his business. She was interested in social class and income. 'I was not averse to a tradesman; but then I would have a tradesman that was something of a gentleman too.' She wanted a man who would wear a sword when he took her to the theatre, not one 'that had the mark of his apron-strings upon his coat'. At last she found what she had been looking for—'this amphibious creature . . . a gentleman-tradesman' and married him. But he overdid the gentleman part, was wildly extravagant, ran deeply into debt and had to escape to France.

A trade card.

A custom-house officer

A custom-house officer figured in one of Moll's escapades during the period of her life when she had turned to crime. She had heard of £300 worth of contraband Flanders lace, stored in a house in London. The officer promised her a reward if she pointed it out to him, which she did. Then came the bargaining over the reward. 'He would fain have put me off with £20; but I let him know that I was not so ignorant as he supposed I was. I asked £100, and he rose up to £30; I fell to £80, and he rose again to £40.' In the end she got £50 and a piece of lace worth £8; but a share of the money had to go to the woman with whom she lodged and who had told her about the lace in the first place.

An author humbly offers his manuscript to a publisher.

Journalists and the Book Trade

Although Moll Flanders met a wide variety of people in the course of her life, her creator, Daniel Defoe, never introduced her to any members of his own profession. She never loved or robbed an author. There is no reason why Defoe should not have put an author into the book as one of the characters; but he did not. A bookseller-publisher (the two types of business were then combined) makes only a brief appearance in *Joseph Andrews* (he firmly rejects the offer of Parson Adams's sermons) and there is nothing to be learned about the book trade in *Tom Jones*. Nevertheless the business of writing and of publishing newspapers and books was one which more and more people were finding profitable and interesting.

Newspapers of a sort were not unknown during the seventeenth century, but censorship restricted them. The history of British journalism begins after the revolution of 1688. Censorship was then abandoned and numerous papers offering news or opinions or both began to appear. The first paper to be published on six days a week was the *Daily Courant* (1702). It was a small sheet, 14 inches by 8, printed on one side only. Defoe started a weekly, *The Review,* in 1704, Steele the *Tatler* in 1709, Steele and Addison the *Spectator* in 1711. (The two last are not direct forerunners of the modern papers bearing these names. No paper of today, except the official *London Gazette,* can claim regular publication since the early eighteenth century. Few even borrow names from that period.)

By 1709 about twenty papers were being regularly published in London, most of them on three days a week, e.g. the *Female Tatler*, the *General Remark*, the *Postman,* the *Postboy,* the *Flying Post,* the *Postboy junior* and the *Whisperer.* 1d or 2d was the usual price. A number of provincial towns had weekly papers, the oldest being the *Worcester Postman* (1690). Advertisements were an important source of newspaper revenue but advertising was not the industry offering well-paid jobs to thousands which it is today. Nor was the cost of advertising high. A paper called *The Generous Advertiser* (1707), charged 3d for every 50 letters and advertisements were collected by the men who delivered the paper.

No one made a fortune out of writing either articles, books or plays. The editor of the weekly *Observator* in 1702 was paid 10s. 6d. for each number. Such people not only wrote the whole paper but also risked prosecution by the government and attacks by private persons, such as William Thompson, who called on an editor and told him that if he did not print a certain paragraph in his paper that day 'God Damn him, he would cut his Throat, and he had a Penknife in his Pocket for that purpose'. Defoe, Fielding, Richardson and Gay never grew rich. Addison and Steele were men of means and did not have to live on what they earned by writing.

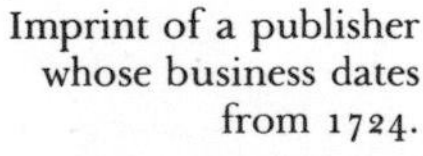
Imprint of a publisher whose business dates from 1724.

Longmans

Grub Street.

Hack writers

Grub Street, a street in the City of London where poor authors lived, had already in the seventeenth century given its name to hack writers and hack writing. The term was now much used. A 'Grub Street' writer meant an ill-paid and usually an unsuccessful writer, whether or not he lived in that particular street. Some booksellers had hack writers on the premises. Fielding, in one of his plays, pictured such a bookseller urging his employees to greater efforts, in spite of the fact that one of them complained he had not dined for two days. Mr. Dash, who specialized in whodunnits, was thought to be slacking.

Bookseller	Well, Mr. Dash, have you done that murder yet?
Dash	Yes, sir; the murder is done. I am only about [i.e. composing] a few moral reflections to place before it.
Bookseller	Very well; then let me have a ghost finished by this day seven-night week.
Dash	What sort of a ghost would you have sir? The last was a pale one.
Bookseller	Then let this be a bloody one.

An example of the lowest level to which a writer could sink can be found in the life of the poet Settle (born 1648), who was so poor in his old age that he wrote comic verses to order in a booth at Bartholomew Fair and in a farce called *St. George for England,* 'acted a dragon inclosed in a case of green leather of his own invention'.

A librarian

Could you do better by looking after books rather than by writing them? There were hardly any public libraries, but a number of valuable private ones existed. Humphrey Wanley (1672-1726) saw his chance here. 'What time he could spare from the trade of a draper, to which his father put him, he employed in turning

'Turning over old manuscripts'.

SOTHEBY'S

FOUNDED 1744

MONDAY, 14th OCTOBER, at 11 a.m. and the following day at 2.30 p.m.

VALUABLE PRINTED BOOKS, FINE BINDINGS, AUTOGRAPH LETTERS AND DOCUMENTS, the property of DR. A. N. L. MUNBY, ESQ., LITT.D., PER DAVIDSEN, ESQ., *of Copenhagen,* MESSRS. MORGAN GRENFELL, and Co., Ltd., and other owners, and books from the Collection of SN. TEODORO BECU, including a collection of English bindings; bindings by Paul Bonet and Pierre Legrain; English literature, including first editions of Francis Meres's *Wit's Treasury,* 1598, and seven works by Milton,

R. H. W. FOWLER, CAPT. CHARLES TREMAYNE, M.C., MRS. E. J. BIGIO, and other owners, and property from the Collection of the late RENE FRIBOURG, of 11 East 84th Street, New York City, including a rare Louis XIV silver-gilt table-spoon and fork, Paris, 1675, a set of four Louis XV table candlesticks by L.-J Lenhendrick, Paris, 1753-4, a pair of Louis XV oval soup tureens, covers and liners by Simeon Gaucher, Paris, 1753, a pair of Louis XVI shallow covered bowls by Henry Auguste, Paris, 1787, a number of eighteenth century French dishes, a Swedish tankard by Rudolf Wittkopf, Stockholm, 1701, a Dutch wine taster by Jacob

Sisley, *Le Bateau Echoué,* 1881, by Claude Monet *Cove, Langland Bay—Le Matin,* 1897, by Alfred *Les Peupliers—Après-Midi à Eragny,* 1899, by Pissarro, *Portrait de la Soeur du Peintre,* 1901, b Picasso, *Jeune Fille à la Rose,* 1907, by Pierre- Renoir, *Vue de Stains—Dans la Banlieue de Par* by Maurice Utrillo. Illustrated Catalogue (13 plat colour), 10s.

WEDNESDAY, 23rd OCTOBER

IMPRESSIONIST AND MODERN PAIN DRAWINGS AND SCULPTURE (immediately

Advertisement of sales at Sotheby's in 1963.

over old manuscripts and copying the various hands, by which he acquired an uncommon faculty of distinguishing their dates.' He became librarian to the Earl of Oxford, and when the British Museum was founded in 1753 the manuscripts which he had looked after formed an important part of it.

An auctioneer

A great man needed old as well as new books to fill his library. The practice of selling works of art and books by auction had been introduced from Holland in 1676. These auctions were held as a side-line by dealers mainly interested in other forms of trade; but in 1744 a bookseller, Samuel Baker, began to hold regular book auctions. His nephew, John Sotheby, later entered the business, which became known as Sotheby's and today auctions books, antiques and works of art from all over the world. Baker auctioned Fielding's books in 1755, the year after his death.

An optician

More reading meant more spectacles. These were supplied by Peter Dollond, who opened an optical workshop in Spitalfields in 1750. Spitalfields was the silk-weaving district of London. Dollond's grandfather had arrived there as a Huguenot refugee from France after the revocation of the Edict of Nantes in 1685. His father, born in 1706, became a weaver too, but he was interested in science and taught Peter optics and mathematics. Peter's business did so well that by 1752 he had set up at 'The Sign of the Golden Spectacles' in the Strand, where he also made telescopes and microscopes. The business he founded still exists as Dollond and Aitchison.

Printers

Spectacles were not yet common. What helped the reader most and increased his pleasure was skilful printing and the use of a clear typeface. This book is set in Baskerville 10 point (i.e. a medium-sized type), designed in the years following 1750 by John Baskerville, who was born the year before Fielding in a Worcestershire village (1706). At the age of twenty he was earning his

Samuel Richardson in 1750.

living as a writing master in Birmingham and became skilled at cutting inscriptions in stone. This led him to the design of type for printing. His new type was not universally popular, but his skill was recognized. Oxford University gave him 200 gns. to design a fount (i.e. a complete set) of Greek type and Cambridge University made him their official printer.

The only eighteenth century designer of type whose fame approaches that of Baskerville is William Caslon (1692-1766). His fount is still frequently used.

This sentence is set in Caslon 10 point, so that you can compare it with Baskerville.

Most printers, however, bought their founts, and did not even cast type, much less design it, themselves. They often combined printing with the publication of books and newspapers. Few wrote books as well, but Samuel Richardson, Fielding's rival as a novelist, managed to.

The printing process had not altered a great deal since its introduction into England 300 years previously. It had not yet been speeded up by rotary presses. Those in use were flat and operated by teams of two men, who could print up to 250 sheets an hour on one side only.

Servants

Steele was not a poor man, but when he stayed at Blenheim, he was appalled by the double line of servants, who stood in the hall expecting a tip (then called a 'vail') as he left. He announced that any of them who came to London might have free seats at his latest play. Other guests, however, had to pay up on such occasions.

It was often said in this period that wealthy people had too many servants and that servants were insolent. The word 'footman', which had previously meant simply 'one who goes on foot' or a foot soldier, took on a new meaning in the reign of Queen Anne. Henceforth it was applied to men-servants, clothed in their masters'

.ISING POPULARITY OF THE HIRED FOOTMAN

3UTLERS WITH £2,000-A-YEAR "BENEFITS"

From Our Special Correspondent

A fire burnt brightly in the hearth, sting arrows of light up to the finely nbered ceiling. Slowly the guests filed st bride and groom. At the slightest 'n of one lingering over his respects, e butler whispered discreetly in his r.

Tactically placed around the oak-nelled hall stood the footmen, resplen-nt in pale blue livery, serving glasses of ampagne. Erect as guardsmen they lanced silver trays firmly with the left nd, the right fast down by the side. In ntrast, the tray borne by your Correspon-nt—in livery for the day—was carried ne too steadily in both.

Weddings are not the only occasions for ich this Paddington firm will supply foot-n. For the past 10 years it has been nding additional staff for house parties some of Britain's stateliest homes. At ner times the footmen will serve at din-rs and cocktail parties but resent any nfusion with waiters who, they point out,

headscarf for the journey back. "The news", said the butler, "reached the master. It is unlikely that they will be invited again."

AVERAGE WEEKLY RATES OF PAY

MALE	FEMALE
Butler, £7—£15	Cook Housekeeper, £5 10s.—£7
Footman, £5—£8	Cook General, £5—£6
Chauffeur: Residential, £10—£12	Nannies, £5—£13
Non-residential, £14—£18	House Parlour Maid, £6—£7
Chef, £15—£20	Housemaid, £5—£6
	Mother's Help, £4—£6
	Lady's Maid, £6—£8
	Parlour Maid, £6—£7

According to Mr. Peter Hunt, a director of a London employment agency, many butlers "have all the benefits of a £2,000 a year man". To their pay must be added free accommodation, keep, free uniform and tips. Several butlers are given a new suit each year, and others can use the fami[illegible]

From *The Times* of 19 March, 1963.

livery (i.e. uniform) who attended the carriage, waited at table and performed numerous personal services. Tom Jones, for instance, had to mount on the back of a footman to be birched. Another of their duties was to keep places at the theatre. When their masters or mistresses arrived the footmen moved to seats in the upper gallery, where they formed a highly critical section of the audience.

Swift is heavily satirical at the expense of footmen. Defoe's anger is directed principally at women servants.

He claimed that some of them had managed to push their wages up from 30s. or 40s. a year (plus their keep, of course) to £7 or £8, and that they were able to dress so smartly that he had kissed one by mistake, supposing her to be a lady. No satirist put the servants' point of view, but Steele wrote in the *Spectator* that 'the general corruption of manners in servants is owing to the conduct of masters'. Sir Roger de Coverley behaved towards his servants with great consideration, except that he would not allow them to sleep in church.

Fielding had a special reason for sympathizing with domestic servants. His second wife was one. In 1749 he opened the Universal Register Office in the Strand, where masters could apply for servants and servants for masters. Joseph Andrews was a footman and a very likable one. (The novel of which he is the hero parodies *Pamela,* by Samuel Richardson. Pamela was a maidservant.)

Slaves

Until 1772 slaves, often West Indian negroes, remained the property of the masters who brought them to Britain as personal servants. They were dressed in elegant liveries and considered an ornament to a house-

hold; but that many ran away in the hope of gaining their freedom can be seen from advertisements in the newspapers, e.g.

> A Slender middle-sized India Black, in a dark grey Livery with Brass Buttons, went from Mrs. Thwaits, in Stepney, the 4th of June, and is suppos'd to be gone on board some Ship in the Downs; whosoever secures and gives notice of him to Mrs. Thwaits, two doors within Aldgate, shall have 10s reward and reasonable Charges.

Occasionally slaves were advertised for sale, e.g.

> A Negro boy about 12 years of age, that speaks English, is to be sold. Enquire of Mr. Step Rayner, a Watchmaker, at the sign of the Dial, without Bishopsgate.

Not all coloured servants were slaves. Dr. Johnson's Jamaican servant Francis Barber was free and the doctor had him educated at Bishop's Stortford Grammar School. Nevertheless there were 14,000 slaves in Britain when a decision of Lord Mansfield, the Lord Chief Justice, at last gave them their freedom in 1772.

The Coal Trade

A footman might be elegantly dressed and have many idle moments, but during cold weather he could not escape from the labour of carrying coal. A big house in the country could use a ton a day for heating and cooking.

In *The Elizabethan Age* there is an account of the various people who made a living out of the coal trade. By the beginning of the eighteenth century more coal was being burned in industry (e.g. brewing, p. 161) as well as in homes; there were now more miners, and more people were employed in transporting coal by cart or ship. By about 1750 Abraham Darby had succeeded in producing coke from coal. This could be used, instead of charcoal, for smelting iron.

Coal was therefore an important, expanding industry

Edwa

Beard the 22d Day of this Instant March bein
at the bottom of a Colepit belonging to Hawksbu
Colework afore said By Accident or misfortu
a Water Barrel dropped down from the Top of
said Pit & Struck the said Edward Beard with s
violence, that he instantly died, And further sa
that the said Barrel was of the value of 5 .

Report of an inquest on a miner killed at the bottom of a 'colepit' belonging to 'Hawksbury Colework aforesaid' (near Coventry). 'By Accident or Misfortune a Water Barrel dropped down from the Top of the said pit and struck the said Edward Beard with such violence, that he instantly died.' (1727).

long before the use of steam for driving machinery became common, in the second half of the eighteenth century. But would a keen eighteenth century father have said to his son: 'You go down the pit, my boy. There's a big future in coal'? No. If the father had been a Newcastle or London merchant with money, advising his son how to make more money, he might well have pointed out the advantages of *investing* in the coal trade. But the profits which came from coal were not passed on to the miners, who remained ill-paid and despised. Those at Kingswood, near Bath, were said to exist in a state of 'bestial depravity'. Their condition and that of other mining villages was a challenge to the Wesleys, whose preaching, hymn-singing and genuine love for the under-dog affected the miners so deeply that tears washed white gutters down their black cheeks.

The keelmen go on strike

The Wesleys helped men and women to endure. They encouraged them to fix their hopes on another world, not to try and change this one. So although they both visited the Newcastle district a number of times, we do not find them urging workers in the coal industry to unite in order to better themselves. But attempts at combination were being made—by the keelmen of Newcastle, for instance.

A 'keel' on the Tyne did the same work as a lighter on the Thames, but by the eighteenth century keelmen did not own their vessels. They were employees of a large organization with fixed rates of pay. However, they realized the necessity of standing by one another. When they said the equivalent of 'Count me in' or 'I'm with you', they used to spit on a stone as a pledge of loyalty. Loyal they were. They managed to organize a strike in 1710 and after some time troops had to be called in to force them back to work. There were no trades unions yet. This was the kind of incident which led to the formation of unions in the following century.

Brewing

Although tea and coffee were becoming fashionable in the first half of the eighteenth century, beer or ale was still the normal drink for men, women and children throughout the country. At that time beer was brewed with hops and ale was not. By the end of the eighteenth century all brewing in this country was done with hops, so the distinction ceased to exist, though some beers of lighter colour are still called 'ale'. In the eighteenth century, however, it was 'porter' rather than beer or ale for which publicans were frequently asked by customers who had the sense not to drink gin. 'Porter' was a thick, dark, bitter beer, first brewed in 1722 and may owe its name to the fact that porters liked it. Anyway it was a beer which proved suitable for brewing in large quantities at a time. This encouraged the building of bigger breweries, particularly in London. Brewing now offered attractive prospects to ambitious young men who had a certain amount of money behind them, and steady jobs to those who had not.

Samuel Whitbread

Samuel Whitbread's father was a gentleman farmer in Bedfordshire. The family must have been tolerably well off since, although Samuel was the seventh child in a family of eight, £300 was available to apprentice him to a London brewer when he left home at the age of 16 in the year 1736. Another £2,600 was provided to help him to set up his own business in 1742. But this good start would not have got him far if he had not worked extremely hard. His daughter wrote:

> In the early part of his trade, he sat up four nights in a week by his Brewhouse Copper, refreshed himself by washing plentifully with cold water, and a clean shirt, and when the state of the Boiling permitted his quitting, retired for two hours to his closet, reading the Scriptures and devotional exercises. When the rest of the world were asleep, he entered on the worldly business of the day, never any ways suffering the Sabbath to be broken into.

In 1750 Whitbread established a brewery in Chiswell Street near Grub Street, and there the firm which he founded still brews beer. It is near Old Street Station in the City of London, not far from John Wesley's house and grave. Truman's is another famous brewing business which dates from the same period.

A stocking weaver

In contrast, here is another career. William Hutton was industrious but poor, and in the early part of his

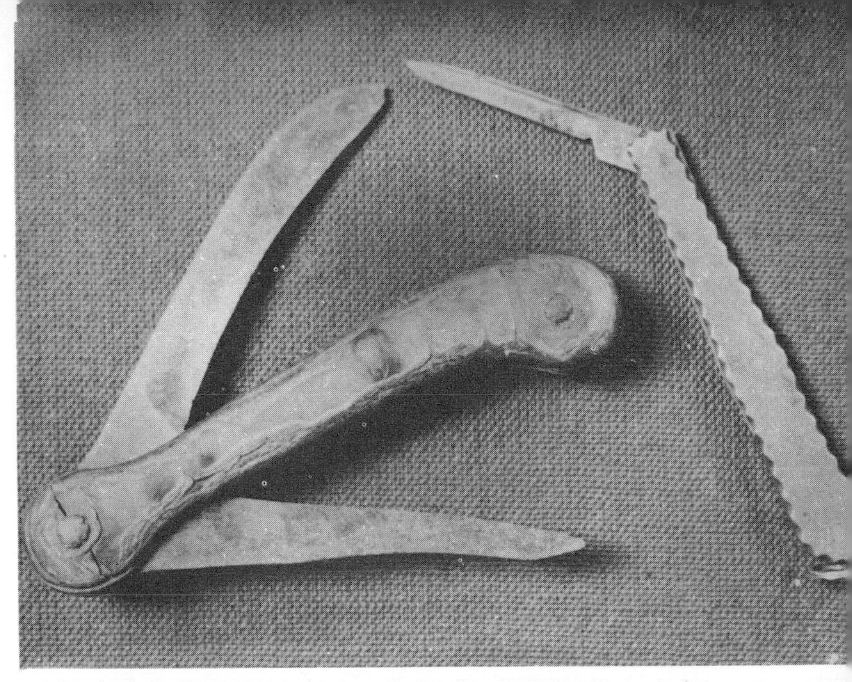

Sheffield had produced cutlery since the 14th century but only in the 18th century did it become more important than London as a producer of knives. Here are a bone-handled pocket knife and a fruit knife made in the early years of the century. It was unusual to have two blades at the same end and opening on opposite sides. The blades have no springs, which explains why the knife could lie half open for the photograph. Two different craftsmen usually made blade and handle, while a third fitted them together.

life he was unlucky. His father was a Derby woolcomber who drank too much and apprenticed William, aged seven, in the Derby silk-mill (1730). This had been built ten years before and was much admired as the first textile mill in England. William found himself the youngest of three hundred workers. 'I had now to rise at five every morning during seven years', he wrote, 'and submit to the cane whenever convenient to the master.'

William's father did not pay for this apprenticeship. It was simply a form of child labour. William's small earnings helped to support his family. At the end of the seven years apprenticeship prospects in silk weaving did not look good, so the boy had to start a second apprenticeship, this time to his uncle, who was a stocking weaver. After another seven years William borrowed £10, bought a stocking frame and set up on his own. But trade was bad and he could not sell any stockings, though he even took them to Leicester, which was already the centre of the stocking trade.

The story ends happily, however, because William Hutton was an exceptional person. He managed to turn from weaving to bookselling, built up a successful business in Birmingham (p. 40) and wrote his own life story.

Entry in a ledger at Coutts's Bank with details of a bill, which they had paid for the Prince of Wales, misspelt Whales, later George II. He had bought a variety of silver, including 'Shaveing Bason'. '2 Tea potts', 'Shugar box'. 'Washball box' [i.e. soap box] and 'Chamber pott'. The weights of each is given in ounces and pennyweights, then their total cost—£374 16s. Charges for engraying are added, making a total of £407 19s. (19s not shown in the photograph.)

1716 The Prince of Whales

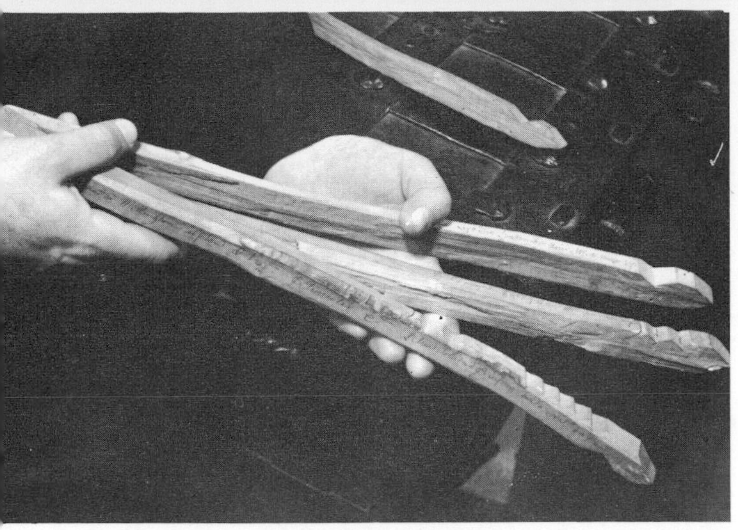

Reckoning by notching a stick called a tally was common in the Middle Ages. By the 18th century tallies were only used by the Exchequer. Those illustrated, which have dates between 1703 and 1707 written on them, belonged to a customer of Martins Bank and were evidence that the Exchequer owed him a considerable sum of money.

The use of tallies by the Exchequer was not discontinued until 1826. In 1834 they were burned. In the process the old Houses of Parliament were set on fire and destroyed.

Banking

In any English town today a number of the solider buildings are banks and the people who work in them as managers or clerks are among the most respected of the local citizens. London bankers, dealing in millions of pounds and with branches all over the world, are among the wealthiest people in the country. In the early eighteenth century not many fathers thought of banking as a profession for their sons. There were few banks in London and fewer still in the provinces. Those at Nottingham, Newcastle and Gloucester were among the earliest. It was only towards the end of the century that banks became common. Our period nurtured the pioneers.

There had been banks in the ancient world and in a few European towns during the Middle Ages. English banking began in the seventeenth century. There was more money in the country as a result of the growth of foreign trade since Elizabethan times and the Civil Wars made people anxious about how to keep money safe. The Tower of London was used by certain merchants, but when in 1640 Charles I seized £130,000 which had been deposited there, it was clear that a safer place was needed. Goldsmiths now acted as bankers, since they had safes and strong rooms.

Hoare's Bank

Hoare and Co., who still do business in London, started as goldsmiths. There were no printed cheques. A cheque was simply a short letter to the goldsmith. One of the earliest is dated 11th July 1676 and reads:

Mr. Hoare,

Pray pay to the bearer hereof Mr. Witt Morgan fifty-four pounds ten shillings and ten pence and take his receipt for the same. Your loving friend

Will Hale

54/10/10

for Mr. Richard Hoare

at the Golden Bottle in Cheapside.

However, the goldsmiths had their difficulties too. They lent large sums to Charles II, which were not paid back. Dissatisfaction with goldsmiths was one of the reasons for the foundation, in 1694, of the Bank of England. This did not prevent private persons competing; but banking in the eighteenth century ceased to be confined either to goldsmiths or to London. Provincial business men, particularly Quakers, became interested.

Lloyds Bank

Sampson Lloyd (1699-1779) came from a family of Quaker iron-founders in Birmingham. At the age of seventeen he was apprenticed to a Quaker merchant in Bristol. After some years he returned to the family business in Birmingham, where he married the daughter of another successful Quaker iron-founder. The iron trade prospered during the Seven Years War (1756-1763), but in the harder times which followed Sampson Lloyd looked for new openings. He had talks with John Taylor. Taylor was not a Quaker but he was a nonconformist—a Unitarian. He had started in Birmingham as a craftsman cabinet-maker and then went into partnership as a maker of buttons and japanned goods (i.e. articles made of metal or wood and lacquered in Japanese style). This business was very successful and Taylor was now a wealthy man and a property owner. In the year 1765 Lloyd, Taylor and Lloyd's son founded the business which is still called Lloyds Bank. Do not confuse it with Lloyd's, the insurance corporation, (p. 196).

Barclay's Bank

In 1736 the Quaker James Barclay entered the London bank which had been established by his father-in-law, also a Quaker, towards the end of the previous century. Thus Barclay's Bank began. At about the same time as the first Barclay entered the business, their banknotes began to be printed. Previously each one had been written by hand. By the middle of the century there were between twenty and thirty banks in London.

Unlucky apprentices

Few apprentices were as fortunate as Samuel Whitbread or Sampson Lloyd. Some were so ill-treated by their masters that they applied to the magistrates for their discharge. Here are some examples:

Joseph Vincent was discharged from Peter Bingham, baker, because he had been cruelly treated, e.g. he was barefoot and his master only gave him 6d. for shoes, which was not enough to buy a pair.

Sarah Gibson was discharged from Joanna Worthington, dress-maker, because instead of being taught the trade she had been made to do housework, had been immoderately beaten and had not been allowed enough food.

Samuel Wood was discharged from James Heley, goldsmith, because he had not been instructed in the art of a goldsmith or buckle-maker, but 'was wholly employed in drawing potts of drink and carrying the same out to customers'.

Among other artisans mentioned as having ill-treated or neglected their apprentices were a framework knitter, a sailmaker, a bricklayer, a writing-master and a peruke-maker.

Watchmaking

The 'domestic system' (work at home) was still the usual way of producing goods during our period. The factory system began in the second half of the eighteenth century. Do not, however, picture every craftsman as his own master, producing a finished article for sale. For instance, watches and clocks, which were now much in demand both at home and for export, were the product of many trades. The movement-maker forged the wheels, which were then shaped by the cutler; steel pinions, springs and chains were all made by separate craftsmen; a gilder gilded the brass wheels, dial-plate enamellers, casemakers and jewellers all did their bit and a finisher assembled the parts.

It was a Doncaster clock-maker, Benjamin Huntsman, who invented a method for making purer and harder steel (1750). He was persuaded to settle in Sheffield,

Watch of 1750, with gold dial, silver hands and a gold case, on the back of which is the goddess Diana.

where his invention enabled the town to take the lead in the steel trade.

The silk trade

In the silk trade, which had grown up in the Spitalfields district of London since the immigration of the Huguenots from France at the end of the seventeenth century, there was first the importer who bought silk from Italy or China. From him it passed to the throwster, who twisted or threw the raw silk into thread. (The throwing of silk corresponds to the spinning of cotton.) The next to handle it was the dyer; then a master weaver bought it and distributed it to journeyman weavers. Their finished work was sold to the mercer, who sold it to the public. It might then provide work for another series of craftsmen or women before starting life as a dress, a coat or a pair of breeches.

Shoemaking

In shoemaking it was possible to set up on your own in a garret, using leather ready shaped by a currier or leather-cutter; but this way of working was strongly opposed by the members of the Cordwainers' Company who found it profitable to work on a bigger scale. They employed different men for each of the three stages of making—cutting out the uppers, closing them and adding sole and heel. They kept shops where shoes were sold ready-made or could be ordered to measure. Some specialized in men's shoes, some in women's, some in shoes for children, some in the peculiar type of shoe worn by chairmen, and one in shoes 'for such persons as have distorted feet'. The members of the Cordwainers' Company did not, however, succeed in getting the one-man shoemakers suppressed.

A complaint against irregular pay and bad conditions in the navy.

A

PROJECT

For MANNING

His MAJESTY's

ROYAL NAVY.

I.

WHilst dull *Projectors* toil in vain
To *man* the Royal Fleet,
And all their *Schemes* contriv'd with Pain,
Such Opposition meet;

II.

Methinks how easy were the Thing,
By Methods worthy *Freemen*,
Both for the Honour of the *King*,
And Service of the *Seamen*.

III.

Nor is my *Scheme* at all confus'd,
For no *Bye Purpose* made;
Let them like English Men *be us'd*,
And regularly paid.

Women's work

Upper and middle class women did not usually take jobs. The professions were not open to them as they are today, and they had not yet been recruited to work in the mines; but a visitor to the Birmingham neighbourhood in 1741 found women working side by side with their husbands in blacksmiths' shops. They made nails.

Wives often did different jobs from their husbands, as is shown by this list of London couples:

Husband	*Wife*
Sells milk	Sells fruit
Watchman	Sells cakes and gingerbread
Soldier in the Guards	Keeps a milk-cellar
Match-cutter	Stay-maker (daughter sells matches)
Waterman	Keeps a public house
Perriwig maker	Quilter of petticoats
Carpenter	Makes cloaks
Cabinet maker	Keeps a grocer's shop
Surgeon	Keeps poulterer's shop
Inlayer of tortoise shell (formerly schoolmaster in a man-of-war)	Keeps a herb shop

Wages, hours and holidays

Wages did not change very much during our period. A labourer might earn about 10s. a week, while members of a skilled trade, such as printers, might earn £1. A quick worker in a skilled trade (e.g. jeweller, maker of optical instruments, chair-carver) might make up to £3 or £4.

Most working hours were not regulated by law. An exception were those of tailors which were fixed in 1721 at 6 a.m. to 8 p.m. with an hour for dinner. During periods of court-mourning, when great numbers of people needed new black clothes quickly, tailors were allowed to work at night as well. 6 a.m. to 8 or 9 p.m.

'Husband—Soldier in the Guards' pictured by Hogarth. The soldier is about to march north to fight the rebels of 1745. Behind an officer kisses a milkmaid while someone steals her milk.

was a normal working day for most craftsmen in London. The building trades worked from 6 a.m. to 6 p.m. or during daylight. Shipbuilding hours were ruled by the tides. Ropemakers were affected by weather. A sunny day was no good to them. They preferred to work through the night.

Shops were open from 7 a.m. to 8 p.m. Washerwomen had perhaps the worst hours of all. They arrived about midnight at their employer's house and worked through the night and the following day.

Artisans on piecework rates could of course earn more by working even longer than the usual hours. This was sometimes necessary to make up for periods of unemployment.

A six-day week with holidays only at Easter, Christmas and Whitsun was usual, but many Londoners took a holiday on each of the eight days in the year when there were hangings at Tyburn (p. 222). They thought such occasions fun.

CHAPTER VI

FUN

WHEN THERE were no hangings, how did people amuse themselves?

Drink helped—wine, beer, gin, coffee and tea. Warmed by these, a man was ready for other pleasures. For instance:

> It was Mr. Western's custom every afternoon, as soon as he was drunk, to hear his daughter play on the harpsichord.

Tom Jones, on the other hand, sometimes thought it best to drink no more than half a bottle and thus kept sober enough to be able to read in bed. One evening the eccentric barber-surgeon-schoolmaster, Partridge, with whom he had been sharing a bottle of wine, offered to lend him *Ovid* (in Latin), a volume of the *Spectator*, Pope's *Homer*, a Roman History or *Robinson Crusoe*—all of which Partridge apparently considered to be normal bedside books for a gentleman. The schoolmaster was a simple soul and knew nothing of a new sort of book, the novel, particularly the French novel, which was beginning to be popular. Nor had he ever been at a play. Later, when Jones took him to see Garrick in *Hamlet* at a London theatre, he was terrified by the ghost.

Puppets

Puppets were more in Partridge's line. One evening, while Jones and he were travelling in the west of England

Squire Western and Sophia (Susannah York).

during their search for Sophia Western, they heard the beat of a drum. Partridge panicked. He was certain they were about to be overrun by the troops of the Young Pretender. It was 1745 and no one knew for certain how far south the Scots had marched. However, the drummer turned out to be advertising a puppet show, whereupon Partridge insisted on watching. 'I love a puppet-show of all the pastimes upon earth,' he said.

The show was an abridged version of *The Provoked Husband* by Vanbrugh. Only 'the fine and serious part' of the play was being performed, according to the puppet-master. A mother who saw the performance said she would bring her daughters next day. On the other hand the maid at the inn where the show had been given, was later found kissing the puppet-man's assistant and excused herself by saying she had learned this improper behaviour from the people in the play. The landlady, her employer, then turned upon the puppet-man and his assistant, called them 'lousy vermin' and ordered them to leave next day. 'I will tolerate no more such doings,' she said. 'It is only the way to teach our servants idleness and nonsense. I remember when puppet-shows were made of good scripture stories, as Jephthah's Rash Vow, and such good things, and when wicked people were carried away by the devil. There was some sense in those matters; but as the parson told us last Sunday, nobody believes in the devil nowadays.'

Arguments about whether young people behave badly because they see bad behaviour on the stage (or on television) still go on.

Practical Jokes

Where no puppets or theatre were available and a majority of the company were incapable of serious conversation, practical jokes were a convenient way of getting through the evening. Parson Adams, during his journey with Joseph Andrews, had the misfortune to spend the night at the house of a bachelor squire of forty. This man was a Member of Parliament and as a young man had toured for three years in Europe; but he remained a boor and was surrounded by boorish companions—'an old half-pay officer, a player, a dull poet, a quack-doctor, a scraping fiddler, and a lame German dancing-master.'

The following are examples of the jokes played:

Joke 1 While Adams was saying grace, the captain removed his chair, so that when the parson tried to sit down he fell on the floor.

Joke 2 While Adams was drinking the health of his host, the poet overturned a plate of soup into his lap, pretended it was an accident, kept apologizing—this was thought very funny—and kept being consoled

Joke 7. Adams is made to fall into a concealed tub of water.

by Adams, who thought it really was an accident—this was thought funnier still.

Joke 3 The footman was ordered to put gin into Adams's ale without his noticing.

Joke 4 The poet recited some uncomplimentary verses about Adams, beginning:

> Did ever mortal such a parson view,
> His cassock old, his wig not over-new?

Joke 5 While the fiddler played, the dancing-master tried to make Adams dance a minuet.

Joke 6 Meanwhile the captain quietly pinned a firework to the parson's cassock and set it alight. It went off with a series of bangs which sent Adams jumping round the room. Everyone roared with laughter and said he was the best dancer they had ever seen.

A trip to Oxford

Although Moll Flanders spent much of her life among criminals, her recreations, when she could afford them, were elegant. One day she was asked by her draper husband (p. 148) if she would like a week's holiday:

'Ay, my dear,' says I; 'whither would you go?' 'I care not whither,' says he, 'but I have a mind to look like quality for a week; we'll go to Oxford,' says he. 'How,' says I, 'shall we go? I am no horsewoman, and 'tis too far for a coach.' 'Too far!' says he; 'no place is too far for a coach-and-six. If I carry you out, you shall travel like a duchess.' 'Hum,' says I, 'my dear, 'tis a frolic; but if you have a mind to it, I don't care.'

Well, the time was appointed; we had a rich coach, very good horses, a coachman, postilion, and two footmen in very good liveries; a gentleman on horseback, and a page with a feather in his hat upon another horse. The servants all called him my lord, and I was her honour the Countess, and thus we travelled to Oxford, and a pleasant journey we had; for, give him his due, not a beggar alive knew better how to be a lord than my husband. We saw all the rarities of Oxford; talked with two or three fellows of colleges about putting a nephew, that was left to his lordship's care, to the university, and of their being his tutors... And thus having lived like quality indeed, as to expense, we went away for Northampton, and, in a word, in about twelve days' ramble came home again, to the tune of about £93 expense.

Moll also liked Bath (p. 39), though she found it slow during the winter, when the fashionable world had returned to London. Other spas outside London were Tonbridge, Cheltenham, Harrogate and Scarborough. At the last sea bathing was recommended—for health rather than for fun. Brighton, a fishing village in Defoe's time, was a fashionable resort by 1750. There too sea bathing was beginning to be recommended by doctors, and the sea-water was also drunk.

St. Bartholomew's Fair

Later in her life, when she had become a thief, Moll Flanders visited, for professional reasons, the annual fairs at Stourbridge, near Cambridge, and at Bury St. Edmunds. At Bartholomew Fair at Smithfield in London she met a well-dressed man who bought her a raffle ticket and took her out in a coach for the evening. They went to the Spring Garden at Knightsbridge and had some drinks. Later the gentleman fell asleep in the coach. Moll then took his gold watch, his silk purse

Vauxhall Gardens, 1751.

Peepshow: 'The siege of Gibraltar'.

full of gold coins, 'his fine full-bottom periwig and silver-fringed gloves', his sword and his fine snuff-box. When the coach had to stop in a narrow street to let another coach pass, Moll slipped quietly out.

It was a pity that her business acumen prompted Moll to leave St. Bartholomew Fair so soon. There was much to be seen there and as a rule only three days in which to see it (Aug. 23-25). The City authorities tried to enforce this limit because, although they and St. Bartholomew's hospital made money from the fair, it had an evil reputation. Thieves did well out of it, heavy gambling led to fights, it kept people awake at night, held up traffic during the day and corrupted honest citizens by the entertainments it provided.

It is true that Bartholomew Fair, unlike Stourbridge, was no longer important for trade—its original purpose—and had become the equivalent of a modern Bank Holiday fun fair. But the entertainment provided was varied. There were no opportunities for making yourself sea-sick or giddy such as a modern amusement park provides. You cannot do much in that line without steam-power or electricity, though 'whirligigs', worked by hand, and at this period beginning to be referred to as 'merry-go-rounds', had been available at fairs

The 'up-and-down' and a vendor of hot sausages.

since the Middle Ages. There was also a crude ancestor of the Big Wheel. (The illustration, though contemporary, is inaccurate. There should of course be four seats.)

Bartholomew Fair shook the soul more than the body. There was every kind of entertainment, from West End theatrical companies to the crudest puppet shows. Here the innkeeper's wife (p. 175) could have enjoyed a puppet performance of *Jephthah's Rash Vow* (the climax of which was the sacrificing of Jephthah's daughter—see *Judges*, Chapter II); but here also she could have seen Fielding's plays. West End theatres closed during the Fair and their companies moved to Smithfield.

All this sounds harmless enough. No modern fair can boast of performances by a West End company, or indeed of any theatrical performances at all. What was the trouble? It seems that amongst the large number of stage shows at the fair many were coarse and some held up the government to ridicule. It was difficult to control what went on. The government viewed it all with suspicion. But to the display of dwarfs and of people afflicted with extraordinary deformities there was no official objection. The advertisements for such creatures give the impression that they were under royal patronage, though in fact the phrase 'By His/Her Majesty's permission' simply meant that the showman had obeyed the law and bought a government licence. Notice that since houses were not numbered till 1770 directions had generally to be given by reference to an inn, which there was no difficulty in finding, e.g.

A conjuror's booth.

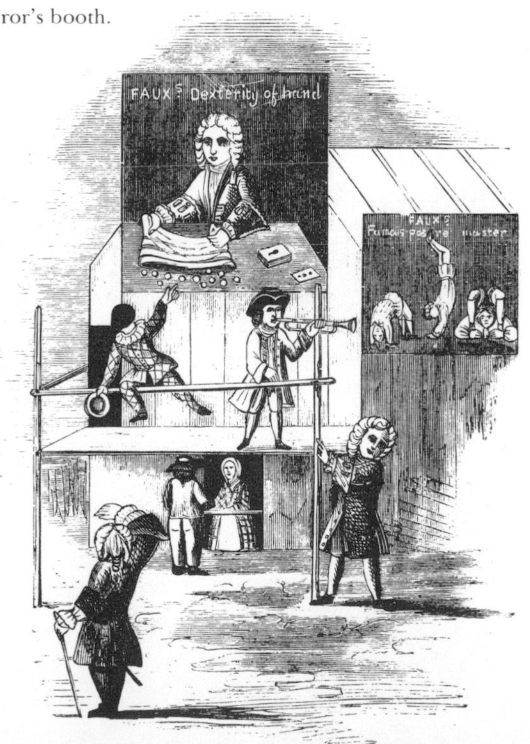

By His Majesty's Permission

Next Door to the King's Head, *in* Smithfield, *during the time of* Bartholomew Fair.

For the Satisfaction of all curious enquiries into the Secrets of Nature, is to be seen a Woman Dwarf, but Three Foot and one Inch high, born in *Sommersetshire*, and in the Fortieth Year of her Age, who discourses excellently well, and gives great Satisfaction to all that ever saw her.

Note, there is neither Loss of Time, or any other inconveniency in viewing this Mistery of Nature.

VIVAT REX.

Further examples were: a man eight foot high, a woman with three breasts, a cock with three legs, an elephant that fired a gun and 'a little black hairy *Monster*, bred in the *Desarts of Arabia*, a natural Ruff of Hair about his Face, walks upright, takes a Glass of Ale in his Hand, and drinks it off; and doth several other things to admiration'.

There were booths containing waxworks and booths in which you could drink while being entertained, for instance by

...a Woman that dances with Six Naked Rapiers, that we Challenge the whole Fair to do the like. There is likewise a Young Woman that Dances with Fourteen Glasses on the Backs and Palms of her Hands, and turns round with them above an Hundred Times, as fast as a Windmill turns; and a Young Man that Dances a Jigg incomparably well, to the Admiration of all Spectators.

VIVAT REX

May Fair

A fair held in May each year, north of Piccadilly, gained an even worse reputation than St. Bartholomew's in spite of being close to a fashionable residential area

Fair on the frozen Thames 1716.

(p. 18). It was finally prohibited in 1709. The district where it was held is still called Mayfair and still has a reputation for wealth and gaiety.

The sights of London

'Seeing the sights' today usually means looking at old buildings or excavations. A sightseer in early eighteenth century London might visit Westminster Abbey and the Tower (because it contained a zoo) but he was more interested in new buildings, such as those described in Chapter I, especially St. Paul's. He liked curiosities and monsters similar to those which were concentrated for short periods at the fairs. There was no 'What's on in London' at the time, but the newspapers contained plenty of advertisements, e.g. of the Lincolnshire Ox, 'Nineteen Hands High and Four Yards Long, from his Face to his Rump'; or of 'an old She *Dromodary*, being seven foot high and ten foot long, lately arriv'd from *Tartary*, and her Young One, being the greatest Rarity and Novelty that ever was seen in the three Kingdoms before'.

In the eighteenth century Greenwich Hospital was still a home for retired seamen.

There were waxworks in which the figures moved. You could see the execution of Charles I in wax '. . . wonderfully Diverting to all Lovers of Art and Ingenuity'; and you could have yourself modelled in wax, 'on reasonable Terms'. There had also arrived recently from Germany a 'moving picture', which was in fact a complicated mechanical toy in which coach-wheels revolved, a huntsman blew his horn, travellers moved along a road with their animals and ships put to sea.

Foreign dignitaries are at once themselves sightseers and part of the sights of London. In 1710 four American Indian chiefs were entertained at Queen Anne's expense.

She ordered that they should be shown 'what is remarkable here', as a result of which they visited, in a royal barge, Greenwich Hospital (p. 184) and Woolwich Dockyard on one day, and on another the Whitehall Banqueting Hall (p. 18); on a third day they were present at a review of cavalry and infantry in Hyde Park.

'Passive' Sport

A preference for watching or talking about sport, rather than taking part in it, is not peculiar to the twentieth century. In fact it is opposition to what one might call 'passive' sport (e.g. by the encouragement of organized games or by tests of endurance and initiative) which is modern. In the eighteenth century, when, in contrast to today, only a minority of the population lived in towns, they could walk into the country without difficulty, and go fishing or rabbit-snaring too, if they liked. Furthermore the sheer business of living gave all but the fairly rich as much exercise as they needed. Hours, as we have seen, were long, and your two feet were the most usual form of transport.

'Passive' sports today are organized on a grand scale. The eighteenth century had no 'gates' of 50,000; but it far surpassed the twentieth in cruelty. Bear-baiting was still practised, though it was dying out; bull-baiting was popular, but cock-fighting was even commoner. The cocks wore spurs and a part of the entertainment was the placing of bets on the winner.

Horse-racing of a sort had been popular at least since the time of Henry VIII. James I and the two Charles's started it at Newmarket; but it was during the early eighteenth century that the sport became organized and that England began to establish her position as the leading racehorse-breeding country. The first Racing Calendar was printed in 1727. There were already enough race meetings to make such a list worthwhile. Publication has continued ever since. In 1740 Parliament enacted the weights which horses had to carry.

The Jockey Club was founded in 1750 to regulate racing at Newmarket, but its authority later covered racing throughout the country. As to the horses, all English thoroughbreds are descended from three Eastern horses, the Byerly Turk, the Darley Arabian and the Godolphin. The Byerly Turk was imported towards the end of the seventeenth century, the Darley Arabian in 1704 from Aleppo and the Godolphin about 1728 from Paris.

Active sport

Stag-hunting was on the decline. 'Hunting' in the early eighteenth century usually meant hunting the hare. Parson Adams, asleep in the open air during his wanderings with Joseph Andrews, had an uncomfortable awakening when a hare was caught within a few yards of him, 'and the hounds, in devouring it, and pulling it backwards and forwards, had drawn it so close to him, that some of them laid hold of the skirts of his cassock, others at the same time applying their teeth to his wig'.

Squire Western hunted both foxes and hares. He loved his beautiful daughter Sophia almost as much as his dogs (Fielding calls them 'dogs', not 'hounds'). As he did not like to be separated for long from either, he made Sophia go hunting with him. There was nothing extraordinary about a woman hunting. Queen Anne had loved it as a girl, and so had Lady Mary Wortley Montagu in her sixties. When she was younger, she was not so keen; neither was Sophia, who only hunted from a sense of duty. She wanted to keep an eye on her father and see that he did not take too great risks. However, her constancy was rewarded when she was thrown from her horse into the arms of Tom Jones.

Tom Jones out after partridge. A horn for powder is slung round his neck.

It is worth noting that it was his dogs and not his horses which took first place in the Squire's affections. It was quite usual for a country gentleman to keep a small pack of hounds. Sometimes these packs hunted a fox; there was nothing new about that; occasional foxes had been hunted for centuries; but at some time during our period, perhaps about 1730, hounds began to be trained for fox-hunting only. In Leicestershire from 1753 Mr. Hugo Meynell hunted fox-hounds in the Quorn country. This was the beginning of fox-hunting as we know it; but neither horses nor hounds were as fast or as keen-scented as they are now.

Hunting the fox was more strenuous than hunting the hare. Addison, after describing Sir Roger de Coverley's enthusiasm for sport, ends by saying that, as old age came on, he left off fox-hunting; 'but a Hare is not yet Safe that Sits within ten Miles of his House'.

In 1750 a Smithfield saddler was advertising 'a new velvet hunting cap (and also a neat light sort for ladies), without seam or button, in one entire piece of velvet, which will not rip and the skull of it is so stout as to defend the head from either fall or blow'. Red coats and top hats had not yet become the fashion; but the idea of a special uniform for hunting dates from the mid-eighteenth century.

Sir Roger de Coverley had shot 'many thousands of Pheasants, Partridges and Woodcocks', and it was the shooting of a partridge on Squire Western's land that brought Tom Jones into serious trouble, while he was still a boy. Guns were not yet very accurate. It was rare to shoot a bird on the wing. A hawk might be more successful than a marksman; but hawking was now uncommon. As an alternative, partridges could be stalked by dogs and then caught in a net.

A net was also used for catching birds at night. A lantern was held behind it, the bushes were beaten, and the birds immediately made for the light. They were then trapped in the net. This was called 'bird-batting'. One night during his wanderings Parson Adams met 'a set of young fellows' engaged in this sport. Unless these young fellows had an income of £40 a year, the Game Act made it illegal for them to kill game. They may have been after smaller birds or they may have been poaching. It seems very unlikely that they can have had the income necessary to bring them within the Act.

Fights

Was fighting fun? For spectators, undoubtedly. A sword fight or a boxing match between men was as entertaining as a fight between cocks with spurs. These were not fights to the death but the spectators expected to see some bloodshed for their money. Often they saw a great deal. Blood and betting were what they had come for.

But how about taking part in a fight oneself? All classes were ready to do so. Apprentices still armed themselves with cudgels (stout sticks), and every male was ready to use his bare fists. A quarrel between boys in the street was thus described: 'First each pulls off his neckcloth and waistcoat while a ring of spectators forms. Then they begin to brandish their Fists in the Air; the Blows are aimed all at the Face, they Kick one another's Shins, they tug one another by the Hair, etc.' But certain rules were observed. 'He that has got the other down may give him one Blow or two before he rises, but no more.' Finally, 'The Father and Mother of the Boys let them fight on, and hearten him that gives Ground or has the Worst.'

A gentleman might use his fists, e.g. to fight a coachman in a dispute about a fare; but to fight another gentleman, he used his sword. Duels were illegal, but were often fought, and fought to the death. Pistols as well as swords were sometimes used, though if one of the pistols was aimed straight there was no need for the swords.

Football and cricket

Modern football had not yet developed. The rough game with few rules which had been played in the streets at holiday time since the Middle Ages was still popular. Cricket however was becoming more like the game we know. Before the eighteenth century references to it are rare and it is hard to tell how the game was played.

It has been suggested that royalists, who kept away from London during the Commonwealth and had time on their hands, took an interest in the bat and ball game which was popular in some villages, particularly in Kent, and began to make it fashionable after the Restoration.

Certainly in the reign of Queen Anne cricket matches with eleven players a side were played between some southern counties. The gentlemen who encouraged the game did so partly because they wanted to place bets on one of the two sides. But they also played themselves and so did poorer people. During the eighteenth century cricket began to develop into the one active game which men of all classes enjoyed together. No pads or gloves or special clothes were worn. The laws of the game were first written down in 1744. The pitch had to be 22 yards long, as now, but the wicket was 22 inches high by 6 broad (it is now 28½″ × 9″) and there were only two stumps (the third stump and the l.b.w. rule were added towards the end of the century). The dimensions of the bat are not specified. In some pictures of the time it looks like a massive hockey stick. Since bowling was underarm and near ground level, a hockey stroke was the best means of dealing with it.

A Sussex cricket club celebrates its bicentenary by playing in eighteenth century dress, with appropriate bat and wicket.

Nobody played a straight bat. The ball was not very different from that used today.

There were 4 balls in an over and whoever drafted the laws seems to have thought of the ball as feminine, e.g.

If a ball is nipp'd up [hit] and ye striker strikes her again, wilfully, before she comes to ye Wicket, its out.

But on the whole it is the similarity of the 1744 laws to those of today which is their most striking characteristic, e.g.

When ye Wickets are both pitched and all ye Creases cut [the Crease was cut in the turf, not marked white as now], ye Party that wins the toss up may order which Side shall go in first at his option.

If ye Wicket is Bowled down, its Out.

. . . if ye Ball be held before she touches ye ground, though she be hug'd to the body, its Out.

Ye Bail hanging on one Stump, though ye Ball hit ye Wicket, its Not Out.

When both Umpires shall call Play, 3 times, 'tis at ye peril of giving ye Game from them that refuse to play.

Note that 'ye' could still be used for 'the', even in the middle of the eighteenth century, though one 'the' appears above.

In 1744, at the Artillery Ground near Moorgate in London was played what a newspaper described as 'the greatest cricket match ever known'—Kent v. All England. This is the first match of which the full score has been preserved. The Prince of Wales and the Duke of Cumberland, soon to earn the nickname of 'Butcher', were among the spectators. When Kent had only three runs to make and her last two batsmen were in, one of them gave a catch which was dropped and Kent went on to win.

Cricket matches between women were first organized in 1745 but it did not become a women's game. Hambledon in Hampshire already had its ground, overlooked by the Bat and Ball Inn; but the great days of the Hambledon Club were in the latter half of the eighteenth century.

Cricket was beginning to be played in schools. Horace Walpole played at Eton and Lord Chesterfield wrote in one of his letters to his son: 'If you have a right ambition, you will desire to excel all boys at cricket as well as in learning.'

Tennis, rackets and fives

Tennis (not lawn tennis, a game invented late in the nineteenth century) was played, but a tennis court was a large and expensive building. There were not many in the country.

Henry VIII and the Stuarts had been keen players, but it was not and is not a ladies' game. Anne did not play. Of the Hanoverians, Frederick Louis, Prince of Wales, son of George II, enjoyed tennis; but a blow from a tennis, or possibly a cricket, ball is thought to have caused his comparatively early death. He was born in the same year as Fielding (1707) and died three years earlier, in 1751.

Other games which needed a specially built court were rackets, which was a simpler form of tennis, and fives, which was played either with the hands, as now, or with a wooden bat.

Bowls, skating and billiards

Bowls was much commoner than the games which needed a built court, since both villages and country houses could provide the necessary greens. Skating had been popular in London since the Restoration, because Charles II's courtiers had learned it during their exile in Holland. Billiards was played on a big table covered with a green cloth, as today, but in other respects the game was different.

Coffee Houses

A wealthy London shopkeeper in the year 1706 is said to have passed his day as follows:

5.0 a.m.	Gets up. Does accounts and other office work.
8.0	Breakfast on toast and Cheshire cheese, followed by work in shop.
10.30	Calls at neighbouring coffee house for news; then back to shop.
Noon	Dinner at home, over shop.
1.0 p.m.	At the Royal Exchange (successor to the Elizabethan one, burned down in the Fire of London.

	There was a courtyard where merchants met and a gallery with shops).
3.0	Lloyd's Coffee House, for business.
4.0 – 5.0	Shop.
Rest of day	Another coffee house, for recreation. Wine shop for drinks with friends. Light supper.
9.0 or earlier	Bed.

It will be seen that visits to coffee houses were an important part of the daily routine; they were paid for business reasons as well as for pleasure. But coffee houses were primarily places where you went to enjoy yourself.

Coffee had become known in the previous century, when it began to be imported by the ships of the East India Company. The first coffee house is thought to have been one opened in Oxford in 1650 or before. The first in London was Pasqua Rosee's, opened in 1652. The house, in St. Michael's Alley, off Cornhill, is marked by a plaque and you can still buy a variety of drinks there, but not coffee. The new fashion spread quickly, like the fashion for espresso coffee bars after World War II. By the beginning of the eighteenth century there were hundreds of coffee houses in London and they were also to be found in most towns of any size throughout the country. As we have seen, they were used, largely by men (though women often served in them), both for business and for gossip. You could have your letters addressed to a coffee house. There was a good fire in winter and copies of the newspapers and private newsletters could be seen. All this could be had for a minimum charge of one penny throughout most of Queen Anne's reign, though it increased to 2d. in 1712.

'Robinson Crusoe'

About the time of this price increase frequenters of one London coffee house were offered the opportunity of reading, in addition to the usual newspapers, 'an Account of a Man living alone 4 Years and 4 Months in the Island of John Fernando'. This man was Alexander Selkirk, who had been rescued from one of the San

coffee house. Guests read newspapers and smoke pipes. A boy
's out coffee and a woman is in charge behind the counter at the
. She does not seem worried by the two guests who are quarrelling.
of coffee keep hot before the fire and an urn with a tap hangs over
provide hot water.

Fernando Islands off Chile in 1709. Defoe became interested in his story and the result was his book 'Robinson Crusoe' (1719).

Lloyd's

So a best-seller as well as a business deal could be born in a coffee house. Hopes could be buried there too or, at Lloyd's coffee house in Lombard Street, sunk. As well as coffee, Lloyd's provided all the latest shipping news, and also sold insurance against risks at sea.

Lloyd's is no longer a coffee house. It has grown into a corporation which is known all over the world; but insurance against sea risks is still one of its most important activities. *Lloyd's List*, mainly shipping news, has been published continuously since 1734 and is thus the oldest London newspaper except for the *London Gazette*.

Newspapers

Lloyd's List was never light reading but most of the increasing number of newspapers in London and the provinces offered entertainment and advertisements as well as information. Accounts of battles, crimes and executions occupied a good deal of space. Battles and the presence of an invading army on English soil, as in 1745, were a godsend to the press and particularly to northern papers like the *Newcastle Journal,* which usually had to be content with reprinting news from the London papers as soon as they arrived.

Newspapers had not yet become generally recognized as ventilators of grievances or fighters against injustice. They were not full of articles in favour of uniting against employers, or against enclosures, the Game Laws and harsh sentences. Printers were not blind to injustice, but if they championed the poor and oppressed they were liable to rouse powerful opposition. It is not surprising that they played safe. As the *Northampton*

For the Benefit of
The DAUGHTER of the late *Mr. MILLS.*
By HIS MAJESTY's Company of Comedians,
At the THEATRE ROYAL in *Drury-Lane,*
This preſent Tueſday being the 26th of *April,* 1737
will be preſented a Tragedy, call'd
The SIEGE of *DAMASCUS.*
Written by the late J. HUGHES, *Eſq;*
Caled by Mr. *QUIN,*
Eumenes by Mr. BERRY,
Phocyas by Mr. *MILWARD,*
Abudah by Mr. *MILLS,*
Daran by Mr. *CIBBER,*
Herbis by Mr. *TURBUTT,*
Artamon by Mr. *ESTE,*
Sergius by Mr. *WINSTONE,*
And the Part of *Eudocia* by Mrs. *CIBBER.*
With Entertainments of Dancing; particularly,
The *Engliſh Maggot* by Mr. *Villeneuve* and Mrs. *Walter.*
The *Drunken Peaſant* by Mr. PHILLIPS.
And the *Ruſſian* Sailor *by* Monſ. *Denoyer.*

Playbill of a benefit performance in which Colley Cibber took part.

Mercury wrote in 1720: 'publick Reflections may bring an Odium upon the Paper, the Business of which is to amuse rather than reform.'

Plays

Playwrights had to be careful too. Not that they were eager to defend the underdog. Even more than the occasionally idealistic journalists, they considered that their function was to entertain. Then as now one of the important questions for anyone in the entertainment business was: How far can I go? How much sex and cruelty will I be allowed to show or talk about?

Far and away the most successful theatrical production during our period was *The Beggar's Opera* (see p. 21). It is what we would call a musical; lyrics are linked by spoken dialogue. Its leading characters are criminals. On the stage, as in the newspaper, the criminal world was of great interest to the public. (It still is.) John Gay, who wrote *The Beggar's Opera*, did not do so out of zeal for reform of the prison system; but there is an element of satire in his work. For instance, he included a song about bribery in high places. Sir Robert Walpole was notorious for the use he made of bribes to keep his majority in Parliament. The following song was obviously directed at him and might even have been taken as implying an insult to the king, whose minister he was:

> When you censure the age,
> Be cautious and sage,
>   Lest the courtiers offended should be;
> If you mention vice or bribe,
> 'Tis so fit to all the tribe,
>   Each cries: 'That was levelled at me.'

Admission ticket (Gallery 2s.) to a benefit performance for Mr. Milward, the original player of Macheath, who is shown in shackles, torn between his two loves.

Colley Cibber, actor and dramatist.

However both the royal family and Sir Robert saw the show and Sir Robert even laughed heartily at the bribery song. Gay had managed to be 'cautious and sage', it seems. But by 1736, as we have seen (p. 9), Walpole's patience was exhausted. Regular censorship by the Lord Chamberlain was introduced in the following year.

Inside a theatre

The Lincoln's Inn Theatre, where these performances took place, was not unlike a modern theatre. It was an enclosed building, lit by candles, very different from the Elizabethan theatres modelled on inn-yards. Scenery could be shifted. A curtain rose and fell. Girls sold oranges as refreshments, and pretty women now appeared upon the stage. Boys no longer acted the female parts, as they had done in Shakespeare's time. However, little attention was paid to period costume. The ancient Romans in Shakespeare's *Julius Caesar* wore eighteenth century clothes.

The stage extended forward over the area now occupied by stalls. The best seats were in boxes, in the lower two galleries (for the top gallery see p. 157) and on the stage itself. The last were very inconvenient for the actors and David Garrick (1717-1779) got rid of them during the period of his great success as an actor in the latter part of the century. The pit where there were cheap seats, as in the top gallery, was squeezed between the stage and the lowest gallery but did not extend below it.

Most of the seats in the theatre were wooden benches and the only way of booking a place was to send a footman to sit in it or struggle in early yourself. To protect the actors from the rough, jostling crowds, a row of iron spikes ran along the front of the stage at Drury Lane and at Covent Garden. But despite the risks they ran, actors could live long lives, e.g. Colley Cibber (1671–1757), and they were now accepted as respectable members of society.

Music

The increase in hymn-singing referred to in Chapter IV is an indication of improvement in musical taste. It was pointed out however that words rather than tunes have survived. The four best-known pieces of music produced in the first half of the eighteenth century are the *Messiah, Rule Britannia, Sally in our alley* and *God Save the Queen*. The composer of the last is unknown. It first became popular when Londoners were rallying to resist the young Pretender in 1745 and came gradually to be

George Frideric Handel.

Thomas Arne (1710-1778), composer of *Rule Britannia*.

adopted as the National Anthem (there had not been such a thing before). The tune has sometimes been attributed to Henry Carey (1690-1743), who certainly did write *Sally in our alley* and a large number of successful operas and songs.

Handel

Handel (1685-1759), who came to London in 1710, was by far the greatest musician working in England during his lifetime. He wrote many operas, which were performed at the Haymarket Theatre (Covent Garden was not yet the headquarters of opera). His most famous work, the *Messiah,* is an oratorio—a sacred story arranged for performance by choir and orchestra. The first performance was in Dublin in 1741, but it was later sung at Covent Garden. It is said that when George II was present he was so deeply moved by the '*Hallelujah*' chorus that he stood up. Audiences often stand when that part of the *Messiah* is reached, and George II's action may have started this.

Like Sophia Western, when her father was drunk, Handel played the harpsichord, which was then the principal musical instrument, as the piano is today. Among the stringed instruments the violin had finally replaced the viol and the 'cello was now mostly preferred to the viola da gamba ('viol with a leg').

Britton, the coalman

Concerts were given in all sorts of rooms and halls, as they are today, but perhaps the most remarkable were those which took place in a long, narrow, low-ceilinged room, reached by a ramshackle outside stair in Clerkenwell. Thomas Britton ran a one-man business, selling coal from a cart. He kept the coal on the ground floor of his little house in Clerkenwell, leaving the upper floor free for quite a different life. He collected old books and manuscripts; he also collected musicians and persuaded them to play; music-lovers came to listen; Britton's concerts became fashionable. Handel himself was among those who played for him; but not for long. In 1714 the coalman had a practical joke played on him by a ventriloquist and died of fright.

Satire

It may be that references to theatrical censorship and to the timidity of newspapers have obscured the fact that satire flourished. Satire, when you come to think of it, is odd. People pay to have contempt poured upon the human race, or upon their country, or upon their class or upon individuals. The attack must be cruel, or nearly so; it must bring its object into contempt or

A satirical painting by Hogarth from *A Rake's Progress*, which incidentally illustrates the pastimes of the rich. On the left a musician sits at the harpsichord, next to him are a fencing master and a dancing master. A jockey kneels on the floor. The Rake receives them in 'night-cap' and 'night-gown' (see p. 80).

make it ridiculous. If it does not do this it verges upon irony.

A dividing line between irony and satire cannot be precisely drawn, but the difference can be illustrated by example. Fielding's novels are full of ironical passages (e.g. the references to the coach passengers, p. 47), but Fielding was not a satirist. He leaves one with memories of the good-hearted Tom Jones, not with a feeling of contempt for humanity. Very different is the effect of *Gulliver's Travels* (1726) by Jonathan Swift or of *The Dunciad* (1729) by Alexander Pope, to whom Swift had written: 'the chief end I propose to myself in all my labours is to vex the world rather than divert it. . . . I have ever hated all nations, professions, and communities, and all my love is towards individuals.'

Whatever their aims, both writers succeeded in diverting as well as vexing. They can still do both. Enjoyment of *The Dunciad* however depends on knowing a good deal about the literary scene in the 1720's, since it is an attack on the 'dunces' (according to Pope) who were his rivals. *Gulliver* is the greater work. It is perhaps the greatest of English satires and many of us think we have read it (as we think we have read *Robinson Crusoe*) because we were told part of the story as children. In fact few have read it and many should.

'All my love is towards individuals.' To some Swift's sad life story is more interesting than his satirical writing. Part of this story is contained in the *Journal to Stella*, a collection of letters published about twenty years after Swift's death. They show not only what fashionable London was like during 1710-1713, but also what the writer was like, as all good letters should.

Pope was a poet. Swift wrote both prose and poetry. It was he who compared the Grub Street writers to the flea, who

> Has smaller fleas that on him prey;
> And these have smaller still to bite 'em
> And so proceed *ad infinitum*.

It was he who expressed as follows his longing for Hogarth, the satirist who attacked not with words but with paint and pencil (Swift was in Dublin, Hogarth in London):

Tobacco labels.

How I want thee, humorous Hogarth!
Thou, I hear, a pleasant rogue art.
Were but you and I acquainted,
Every monster should be painted:
You should try your graving tools
On this odious group of fools;
Draw the beasts as I describe them;
Form their features, while I gibe them;
Draw them like, for I assure ye,
You will need no *car'catura*;
Draw them so that we may trace
All the soul in every face.

Fielding wrote:

> I esteem the ingenious Mr. Hogarth as one of the most useful Satyrists any Age hath produced.

While Fielding was writing *Tom Jones* and Swift was dying, Hogarth was painting one of his most famous satirical series, 'Marriage à-la-Mode' (1745). Six years later he produced Gin Lane (1751).

Tobacco, snuff and gin

Beer-drinking and the smoking of tobacco in long clay pipes were already pleasures within the reach of all at the beginning of our period (though smoking was not general among women). To these pleasures were added the taking of snuff during Queen Anne's reign and the drinking of gin during the reign of George I.

Snuff is tobacco in powdered form. You sniff a pinch of it up your nose and the sensation, some think, is

Gin Lane, by Hogarth. Huge shop signs jutted out into the streets until they were forbidden under George III, when houses were numbered. Here we see the pawnbroker's, the coffin-maker's and the gin-shop's. Ruined by drink, men and women crowd into the pawnbroker's. At the back a woman is laid in her coffin, while her child cries. One house is collapsing; in another a man has hanged himself. On the right two little girls in charity school uniforms each enjoy their dram and a baby has gin poured down its throat.

pleasant. Large quantities of snuff were captured from Spanish ships during the War of the Spanish Succession and snuff-taking thus became popular among Englishmen. Women also adopted the habit. Steele complained that women would even pass round a snuff-box during the sermon in church, or offer a pinch to one of the churchwardens, when he was taking the collection.

But the best buy was gin. It is a spirit distilled from grain and flavoured with juniper, the French for which is 'genièvre'. 'Gin' is a shortened form of this. The word and the drink became common during the reign of George I, because it had been thought wise at the end of the seventeenth century to encourage the production of cheap English spirits in order to improve the balance of trade. The new drink soon became catastrophically popular. Ale-houses had to be licensed, but anyone could sell gin. In London alone thousands of gin shops sprang up. Their offer to customers was: 'Drunk for 1d, dead drunk for 2d, straw for nothing.' It took many years to check the evil. Neither producers nor consumers wanted to be interfered with. After a number of unsuccessful attempts the government succeeded in putting a duty on gin and a licence for selling it became compulsory, thus opening the way for tea to become the national drink. This was in 1751. In the same year Fielding, who had become a magistrate in 1748 (p. 11), published his *Enquiry into the Causes of the late Increase of Robbers,* in which he wrote:

> Gin is the principal sustenance (if it may be so called) of more than an hundred thousand People in the Metropolis. Many of these Wretches there are, who swallow Pints of this Poison within the Twenty Four Hours; the dreadful Effects of which I have the Misfortune every Day to see, and to smell too.

In short, gin led to the subject of our next chapter—Trouble.

CHAPTER VII

IN TROUBLE

GIN caused poverty and squalor; it was thus indirectly a cause of crime; but you should not picture the underworld reeling to their thefts or highway robberies under its influence. A criminal had to be skilful and alert. Among all the criminal characters in *The Beggar's Opera* only one, Mrs. Diana Trapes, is a regular gin drinker. She liked the best quality. Peachum, the villain—if one can single out a villain in such a rogues' gallery—complimented her on this. 'One may know by your kiss', he said, 'that your gin is excellent.' Mrs. Trapes explained her principles in song:

The life of all mortals in kissing should pass,
Lip to lip while we're young—then the lip to the glass.

She kept her wits about her and earned a good living by the sale of stolen clothing.

Moll Flanders becomes a thief

Moll Flanders was driven to theft by poverty, when she was middle-aged; but she kept sober. She was fastidious in certain matters and for many years refused to use make-up, because she thought she did not need it. Her first theft was not planned. Passing an apothecary's shop in Leadenhall Street, Moll saw a little bundle on a stool in front of the counter. A maidservant was standing with her back to it, while the apothecary's

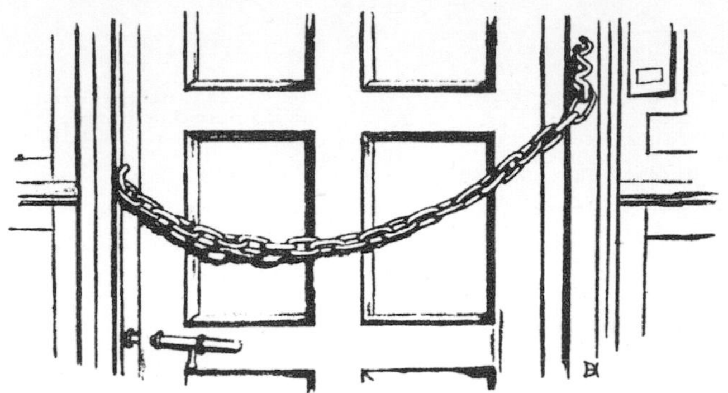

'A criminal had to be skilful'. Chained front door inside Dr. Johnson's house.

apprentice, standing on the counter with a candle in his hand, was looking for something on a high shelf. He too had his back to the bundle.

> This was the bait; and the devil who laid the snare prompted me, as if he had spoke, for I remember, and shall never forget it, 'twas like a voice spoken over my shoulder, 'Take the bundle; be quick; do it this moment.'

Inside the bundle were some baby-clothes, trimmed with fine lace, a silver porringer (one pint), a small silver mug (containing 18s. 6d., wrapped in paper), six spoons, some other clothes and three silk handkerchiefs. Moll never heard who the owner had been. At first she was afraid that the things might belong to some poor widow who had sold them to buy bread for her child. But she needed bread herself and soon yielded to temptation a second time.

Meeting a little girl going home alone from a dancing class, Moll made friends with her and, as they walked along, succeeded in quietly stealing the child's necklace of gold beads, which turned out to be worth £12. Her next haul was a parcel containing fifty yards of silk and eleven yards of velvet, which had already been stolen, but had been dropped by the thieves when they were chased.

Moll now found it convenient to live in the house of a woman who was a receiver of stolen goods. This woman arranged for her to have lessons from a female thief, who specialized in shoplifting and the unhooking of ladies' watches. (These were not worn on the wrist, but at the waist.) Moll and her instructress worked as a pair, one pretending to stumble against the lady while the other came up from the opposite side and

Whereas on Saturday, the 27th Inſtant January, in the Night: a Waggon was robb'd in the Saracen's Head Inn, on Snow-Hill, and were taken out, one Truſs, directed to THOMAS CHANCE of Bromſgrove: One Paper Parcel, directed to Mr. VERNON, of ditto: One Paper Parcel directed to Mr. EDWARD TOY, of Kidderminſter; the Paper Parcels are ſuppoſed to be Writings: Whoſoever will bring the ſaid Paper Parcels and Truſs, to Mr. JOSEPH WINSMORE's, at the Lock and Key, in Smithfield; ſhall receive One Guinea Reward, and no Queſtions asked; of the ſaid Mr. JOSEPH WINSMORE.

Loſt on Wedneſday the 24th of this Inſtant January, A large Red Liver-colour'd Spotted Spaniel Dog, cut Tail, a Notch in each Ear, very fat, and ſmooth coated: Whoever brings him to the Hon. Coll. WILLIAM COSBY, in Soho-Square, or to Mr. ROBERT FOSDICK, at the Hoop and Feathers Tavern in Piccadilly, ſhall have a Guinea Reward, and no Queſtions ask'd.

Advertisements for stolen goods in *The Daily Journal*. Both promise 'no questions asked'.

took the watch. They dressed very well, even wearing gold watches themselves, so as not to look conspicuous among fashionable people. On Moll's first operation they took a watch for which the receiver gave them £20.

This partnership was successful at first. Moll saved £200 and began to think of leading an honest life once more, particularly after her partner had been arrested and hanged. The prospect of what would happen to her if she took a false step, or if her luck turned, frightened Moll; but she could not now change her ways. After going straight for a time, she undertook a particularly heartless and very profitable theft of silver and jewellery from a woman whose house was on fire. Since her partner had been arrested while stealing from a linen-draper's, Moll was now, as she put it, 'very shy of shoplifting, especially among the mercers and drapers, who are a set of fellows that have their eyes very much about them'. Thereafter she stole only from shopkeepers who had just started a business and were inexperienced. But she continued to get richer. When she had saved £500, there was no longer any question of poverty driving her to steal. She had to admit to herself that, in spite of the terrible risks she was running, she now preferred a life of crime. She found that the prospect of imprisonment in Newgate, followed by hanging or transportation, no longer affected her. On the other hand she was not prepared to be burnt at the stake—the penalty for women who counterfeited money. So when some coiners made her an offer of employment, she turned it down. In the end Moll was caught and condemned to death for stealing two pieces of brocaded silk, value £46. She was to be hanged twelve days later, but on the eleventh day friends secured a reprieve. So next morning, when the bell of St. Sepulchre's tolled for six prisoners on their way to Tyburn, Moll was not among them. She was sentenced to be transported to Virginia where, since she had money, she was able to buy her discharge and settle down. She married a retired highwayman.

Highwaymen

'Highwayman' is a word which first appears in the seventeenth century. It means a robber of travellers on the road. There is no comparable word in French or

German, where that sort of man was simply described as a thief or a robber. Only in England did he acquire an inflated name and an inflated reputation.

The Beggar's Opera has a highwayman hero, Macheath. He is betrayed, captured and taken to Newgate. Immediate execution is ordered, the bell tolls, and amid the lamentations of a number of women who claim to be married to him, Macheath sets out for Tyburn. But then he is reprieved.

A clergyman who later became Archbishop of Canterbury criticized *The Beggar's Opera*; he believed that to glamorize a criminal and not even show that he was hanged in the end, would increase crime.

There is no evidence that highway robbery did in fact increase as *The Beggar's Opera* toured the country. Robbery was already frequent and continued to be so. But although John Gay's work did not incite to crime, he does bear some responsibility for establishing the highwayman as a glamorous figure. Macheath has the manners of a gentleman. He several times talks of honour, and the only one of his robberies of which details are given is directed against gamblers on their way home from a gaming house in Marylebone—victims not likely to evoke much sympathy. The female characters in the opera adore Macheath (at least until they find he does not keep his promises), and he adores them ('I must have women. There is nothing unbends the mind like them').

Thus began the legend of the gay devil-may-care type of highwayman who robbed only the rich and was gallant to women. In the following century Harrison Ainsworth, a writer of historical novels, took a real highwayman, Dick Turpin, and built him up into a hero; since when the romantic highwayman legend has been firmly established.

Dick Turpin (1706-1739)

Turpin was in fact an unpleasant character 'distinguished from his early youth for the impropriety of his behaviour, and the brutality of his manners'. He was apprenticed to a butcher of Whitechapel in what is now the east end of London, so that when he married he was able to make ends meet by stealing cattle and cutting up the carcases for sale. Later he joined a gang of Epping Forest deer-stealers. They were not doing very well and decided to go in for house-breaking. There was no question of honour or chivalry. When the gang broke into the house of an old woman, who would not say where she had hidden her money, Turpin sat her on the fire until she spoke out.

The gang's sense of honour did not even cover its own members, since one of them, attracted by the offer of a hundred pound reward, gave evidence against two of his mates, as a result of which they were hanged and their bodies were left dangling in chains as a warning. Turpin however escaped, met a highwayman on the road and went into partnership with him; but the fact that he now robbed on horseback did not make his manners any more gentlemanly. At Bungay in Suffolk he and his partner saw two young women being paid fourteen pounds for a delivery of corn. Turpin decided to rob them of the money. His partner objected, saying it was a pity to rob such pretty girls; but Turpin insisted and got his way.

Robbery eventually led to murder. Essex became too hot for Turpin and he went north. For about fifteen months he made enough money by horse-stealing in Lincolnshire and Yorkshire to live like a gentleman. He was invited by his neighbours to go hunting and shooting. A trivial matter led to his being brought before a magistrate, but once enquiries started, further evidence was obtained and he found himself in York castle, awaiting trial at the Assizes.

Turpin had changed his name to Palmer and nobody in the north realized he was the Richard Turpin who had robbed and murdered in Essex. But his luck now deserted him. He wrote to his brother in Essex asking him to send a letter testifying to 'Palmer's' good character. His brother however was not prepared to pay for the letter (postal charges had at that time to be paid by the recipient) and it was taken back unopened to the post office—probably a local inn where arrangements were not very orderly. Anyhow a schoolmaster called Smith, who had taught Turpin to write, happened to see the letter lying about, and recognizing the hand-writing, took it to a Justice of the Peace, who opened it.

That 'John Palmer' should write in Turpin's handwriting to Turpin's brother was highly suspicious. As a reward for his zeal, poor schoolmaster Smith found himself sent to York to give evidence and this led to Turpin's conviction. He was hanged at York on the tenth of April 1739, in a new coat and a new pair of shoes, which he had bought for the occasion.

'With the greatest good-breeding'

Although less gallant in fact than they are made out to be in fiction, some highwaymen were 'gentlemen' in the sense that they mixed with rich people. They sometimes came from good families themselves. People whom they robbed were prepared to deal with them in a 'gentlemanly' way in order to save themselves trouble and regain their possessions. Here is an example.

Late in the year 1749 Horace Walpole's coach was held up on a moonlight night in Hyde Park. It is true that Hyde Park was then on the outskirts of London, not in the centre, as it is today. All the same, Walpole's

Wealthy spectators are allowed seats on the stage to watch a scene from *The Beggar's Opera.* (*Left to right*) Lucy Lockit, Lockit (*with gaoler's keys*), Macheath (*manacled*) Polly Peachum and her father.

whole journey from Holland House (now W.8.) to his home in Arlington Street (now W.1.) would normally have taken no more than fifty minutes. It is extraordinary that out of all the armies of male servants in the two houses at either end of the journey, it was not possible to furnish a strong bodyguard. Walpole was not unaware of the need for protection. He had written to a friend: 'One is forced to travel, even at noon, as if one was going to battle.' On this occasion however his precautions were not sufficient to prevent two highwaymen from taking his purse, watch, seals and sword, and the watch of his coachman.

In spite of the fact that Walpole had nearly been killed by the pistol of one of the highwaymen, which

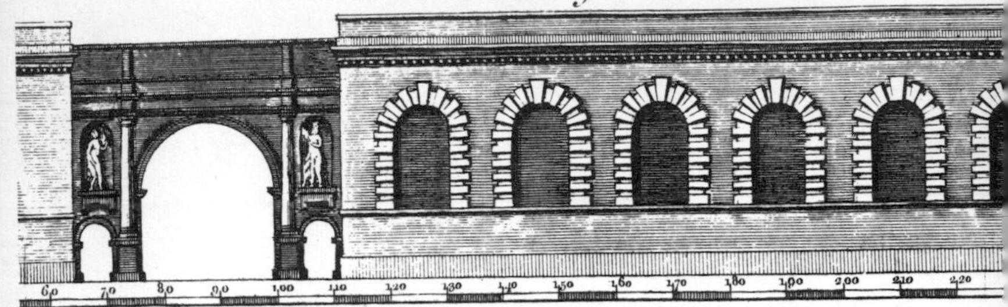

Plan for a new gaol.

had gone off accidentally, he took the whole affair calmly. He advertised in the newspapers, offering £20 reward; the highwaymen replied by letter, offering to return the valuables they had stolen for £40. Naîvely they wrote that they depended on Walpole's honour 'for the punctual payment of the Cash'; but in fact they depended on threats: 'If you shall Deceive us, the Concaquence may be fattall to you.' Walpole stuck to his offer of £20 and this was finally accepted.

One of these two highwaymen was James Maclean, the son of a Scots minister of good family. Maclean had failed in trade and taken to the road. In the summer of 1750 he was captured after robbing the Salisbury coach. Walpole refused to give evidence at the trial. 'The whole affair was conducted with the greatest good-breeding on both sides', he wrote later, referring to the Hyde Park affair. Others, however, took a less generous view of Maclean's activities and he was duly hanged at Tyburn.

Prison

Maclean's last days in prison were alleviated by visits from men and women of fashion, who, like Walpole, bore him no grudge. Most prisoners, although they may have had far less on their consciences than Maclean, had

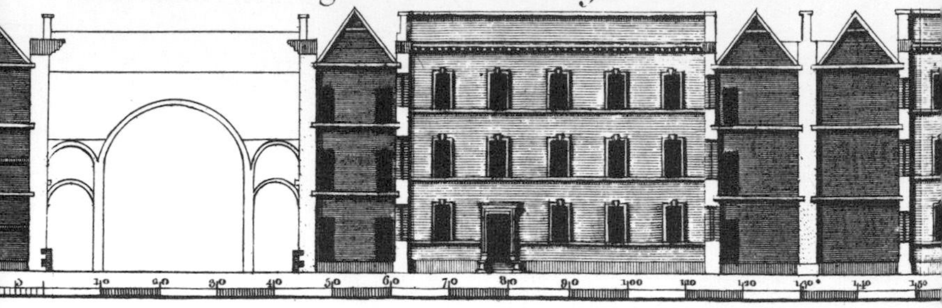

less money in their pockets and therefore existed in a state of semi-starvation and squalor.

'You know the custom, Sir. Garnish, Captain, Garnish.' Thus the gaoler welcomes MacHeath to Newgate, and in the scene which follows it is made clear that the more garnish (money) he is prepared to pay, the lighter will be the fetters attached to his wrists and ankles.

A gaoler had no salary. On the contrary, he had to buy his position. To reimburse himself and make a profit, he squeezed money out of the prisoners. That the gaoler in *The Beggar's Opera* was not simply a caricature was made clear only a year after the show had opened. In 1729, as a result of the efforts of an M.P. called James Oglethorpe, Parliament set up a committee which reported on the scandalous state of the Fleet and Marshalsea prisons in London. There were some dismissals and new gaolers were appointed, but the system remained the same and there was little improvement in conditions. When members of the 'Holy Club' (p. 135) began visiting Oxford prison in 1730, they found that 'garnish' was still levied on the inmates, who were, as one of the Wesleys wrote:

> Compelled since laws and jailers so ordain,
> To pay for misery, and to bribe for pain.

Though the prisons were horrifying, they were not intended as places of punishment or reform. Our modern prison system was developed during the nineteenth century on the basis of ideas formed by John Howard in the last quarter of the eighteenth century. Fines or imprisonment are now the normal penalties; in the eighteenth century the penalty for all except the smallest offences was death or transportation.

Sentences of imprisonment were rare. As a rule prison was simply the place where you waited, first for trial and afterwards for execution, a convict ship to the American colonies or a reprieve. Prison was also the place to which debtors were sent. They could be committed for a small debt, and as they then lost all opportunity of earning, their chances of being able to pay diminished. Many were joined by their families and remained in prison for years, during which time they became indebted to the gaoler; so that even when the original debt was paid or remitted they still could not go free.

From *The Times* of 12 July, 1963.

£40,000 GEM RAI[D] ON DUCHESS'S CAR

BELGRAVIA AMBUSH

A gang led by a coloured ma[n] ambushed a car containing Hel[en] Duchess of Northumberland outsi[de] the home of her son-in-law a[nd] daughter, the Duke and Duchess [of] Hamilton, in Eaton Square, Belgravi[a] yesterday and escaped with a box [of] jewelry believed to be valued [at] £40,000.

The raiders grabbed two boxes [of] jewels from the car. But Mr. Stanl[ey] Woods, aged 43, a guard from Securic[or] the security company, who was wi[th] the Duchess, chased the gang and [re]covered one box after grappling wi[th] a man. Mr. Woods, of Welling, Ke[nt] received a wrist injury.

From *The Times* of 19 July, 1963.

HIGHEST LONDON CRIME LEVEL

GANGS' WIDER USE OF FIREARMS

FROM OUR POLITICAL CORRESPONDENT

A "disturbing" increase in the use of firearms by robber gangs was brought to the attention of Parliament yesterday by Sir Joseph Simpson, Commissioner of Police for the Metropolis, in his annual report for 1962.

He thinks this trend "is typical of the changing ways of the more vicious type of modern criminal", and recommends that penalties for possessing firearms without a certificate should be made much heavier.

Indictable crime reached a higher level than ever before recorded, the Commissioner states.

From *The Times* of 14 June, 1963.

STATE OF PRISONS DENOUNCED

CAUSES OF CANADIAN CONVICT RIOTS

FROM OUR OWN CORRESPONDENT

OTTAWA, JUNE 13

Disgraceful conditions in Canada's federal prisons are considered to be a contributing factor in a number of riots among inmates in the past 18 months.

Bridewell

There was one type of prison where prisoners were usually sent for correction rather than simply for detention. This was the Bridewell, where vagrants and men or women guilty of small offences might be sent to be whipped and provided with some monotonous kind of work, such as beating hemp. The London Bridewell had been opened during the reign of Edward VI in a former royal palace which stood on a site previously known as the Well of St. Bride, near where St. Bride's church now stands.

> This Edward of fair Memory the Sixt,
> In whom, with Greatness, Goodness was commixt,
> Gave this Bridewel, a Palace in old Times,
> For a chastising House of vagrant Crimes.

By the eighteenth century similar institutions, called by the same name, had been built all over the country.

Other penalties

The Reverend Laurence Howel, M.A., who wrote a pamphlet alleging that George I was a usurper, received the following sentence: to pay a fine of £500 to the King, to remain in prison for three years, to find four sureties of £500 each and to be bound himself in £1000 for his good behaviour during life, and to be degraded and stripped of his gown by the hands of the public executioner.

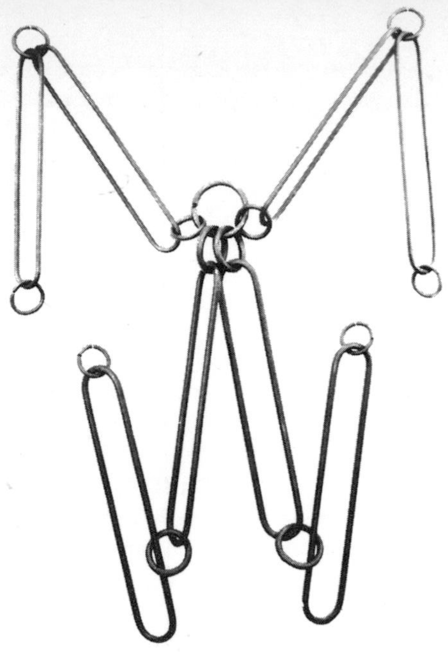

A set of manacles like those worn by MacHeath (p, 215).

Undismayed, he indignantly enquired 'Who will whip a clergyman?' The court answered 'We pay no deference to your cloth, because you are a disgrace to it and have no right to wear it'.

Howel's gown was immediately torn off by the hangman, who was present. He petitioned the King and was not whipped, but he died in Newgate prison before completing his sentence. His case shows that although fines or imprisonment were rare, they could sometimes be imposed.

Some of the ferocious penalties of earlier times (e.g. the boiling alive of poisoners) were no longer lawful; neither was torture, except for *peine forte et dure,* which consisted in laying the prisoner face upwards, with legs and arms outstretched, on a hard floor and piling weights of stone or iron on his chest, so that he could ultimately be pressed to death. This torture was used on prisoners who contrived to avoid standing trial for murder or theft by refusing to plead guilty or not guilty to the charge. In this way they hoped to escape conviction and the confiscation of their property resulting from it. Pressing was inflicted in 1721 and in 1735 and was not abolished until 1772.

The stocks, the pillory (honourably endured by Defoe in 1703 for writing what the government considered a seditious pamphlet) and the ducking stool (for nagging women) were still in use; and convicted persons could be whipped, branded or have their ears cut off. Traitors could still be hanged, drawn and quartered, i.e. they were cut down before they were dead and disembowelled, after which their bodies were cut into quarters. What one authority calls 'the decency due to the sex' resulted in this punishment not being inflicted on women. Instead, when guilty of treason, which in their case included murdering a husband or counterfeiting

The Fleet Prison for debtors in 1691. The man on the left carries a bunch of herbs, because of the smell of the place. The man in the centre puts money in the debtors' begging box.

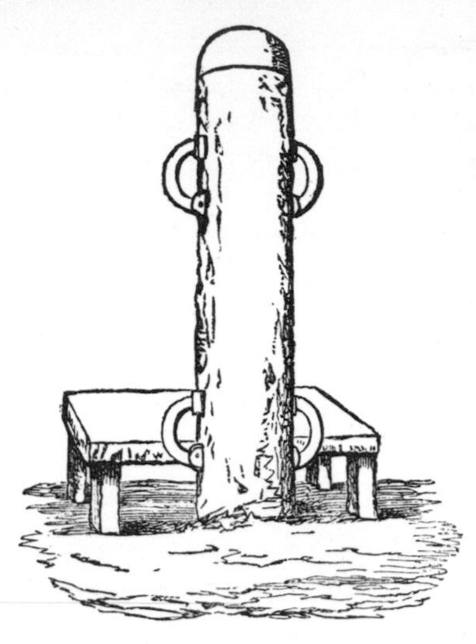

Combined whipping post and stocks. For whipping, the wrists were made fast in the upper iron clasps. When stocks were required the offender sat on the bench and his ankles were made fast in the lower clasps.

coin, women were strangled and burnt at the stake (i.e. they were supposed to be dead before the burning started). A sixteen-year-old girl was burnt at Winchester in 1738, for poisoning her mistress.

Hanging

Hanging had always been a common method of execution, but not a spectacular one. In the past it was the beheading of a noble traitor, the disembowelling of a Jesuit or the burning of a heretic which had drawn the crowds. Only in the eighteenth century did criminals take the centre of the stage. Their public execution, which was intended to deter others by providing a terrible example, became a kind of pageant.

The hanging of criminals at Tyburn (near the Marble Arch) was one of the sights of London. The condemned took trouble to dress well (cf. Turpin p. 214). The men had themselves shaved. There were fewer women because a pregnant woman was never executed and by the

Peine forte et dure ('Hard and grievous punishment').

time her child was born there was a chance that her sentence might be reduced to transportation. Women who failed to escape hanging often dressed in white and wore great silk scarves. They carried baskets of flowers and oranges, which they distributed to the crowds.

The journey from Newgate (near where Gamages and the *Daily Mirror* building now stand) to Tyburn was over two miles. Prisoners of sufficient importance were allowed to travel in a coach, preceded by a hearse (though this privilege was generally refused to murderers). The majority made the journey by cart. There were three prisoners in each cart, each sitting manacled on his or her coffin. The crowds made the journey a slow one, even compared with travel through London today. The two miles took about two hours.

More often than not the spectators were friendly. Fruit and flowers were thrown into the carts and the prisoners were allowed to stop at taverns for drinks, which they were not asked to pay for.

A stop was also made outside St. Sepulchre's church. The great bell of this church was rung on the evening

A Tyburn execution, by Hogarth. The condemned man rides with his coffin in a cart. The clergyman has come in a coach which waits near the triangular gallows (suitable for three simultaneous hangings). Grandstand seats provide a good view for those able to pay.

preceding an execution day and now it was rung again, after a clergyman had prayed for the condemned.

Meanwhile the hangman waiting at Tyburn had not gone thirsty. There was an occasion when a prison chaplain was mistaken for a condemned man by a drunken hangman and found the rope being put round his own neck instead of the criminal's.

Prisoners with money tipped the hangman and he made more money after the execution by selling the bodies back to relatives or friends for burial. Those which were unclaimed were sold to surgeons for dissection; this was carried out in public and drew large crowds.

Fielding disapproved of public executions and the procession to Tyburn. In his 'Enquiry' (p. 207) he wrote:

> The Day appointed by Law for the Thief's Shame is the Day of Glory in his own Opinion. His procession to Tyburn, and his last Moments there, are all triumphant . . . If Executions were so contrived, that few could be present at

them, they would be much more shocking and terrible to the Crowd without Doors than at present, as well as much more dreadful to the Criminals themselves, who would thus die in the Presence only of their Enemies; and where the boldest of them would find no Cordial to keep up his Spirits, nor any Breath to flatter his Ambition.

The procession to Tyburn was stopped some thirty years later (1783) and executions were thereafter carried out in front of the prison, to the chagrin of Dr. Johnson, who commented: 'Sir, executions are intended to draw spectators. If they do not draw spectators, they don't answer their purpose. The old method was most satisfactory to all parties . . .' He need not have worried. Only the procession had been discontinued. Public executions continued to be held in front of Newgate prison and elsewhere and to draw enormous crowds, until 1868.

Juvenile offenders

Readers of this book may be wondering whether, if they had lived in the eighteenth century, their age would have saved them from hanging. The answer is probably: No. Only children under seven were safe from the gallows. As a rule those between seven and fourteen were not sentenced to death, but they could be. In 1748 William York, aged ten, received the death sentence for murder. The judge said:

He is certainly a proper subject for capital punishment, and ought to suffer; for it would be a very dangerous consequence to have it thought, that children may commit such atrocious crimes with impunity . . . Though the taking away the life of a boy of ten years old may savour of cruelty, yet as the example of this boy's punishment may be a means of deterring other children from the like offences . . . the law ought to take its course.

However York's execution was postponed four times and after being under sentence of death for nine years he was pardoned on condition that he went to sea.

Mercy

Children were not the only people who were pardoned. In reading the foregoing pages you may well have felt the need of a few firm figures on crime, such as are to be found nowadays in Whitaker's Almanac. For instance, we learn that in *all England and Wales* during 1961 six persons were sentenced to death. Of these six sentences, one was commuted to life imprisonment, and one reduced to manslaughter on appeal. Four persons were executed.

Neither criminal statistics nor any other statistics were systematically kept until the nineteenth century, but we know the number of those condemned to death *in the City of London and the County of Middlesex alone,* from the year 1749. Here they are, up to the year of Fielding's death:

1749	61
1750	84
1751	85
1752	52
1753	57
1754	50

And here are the numbers of those executed;

1749	44
1750	56
1751	63
1752	47
1753	41
1754	34

Work out the proportion for each year. Mercy tempered the harshness of the law. Some convicts, like Moll Flanders, were transported instead of being hanged. Others managed to obtain a pardon from the King.

Mercy sometimes saved a man before conviction. For

instance, since the death penalty could be imposed for the theft from a dwelling house of goods worth 40s. or more, juries often agreed that 39 shillings was the value of stolen property which should really have been assessed at much more. In such cases each juryman was, strictly speaking, telling a lie; but it was a 'white lie' known as 'pious perjury'.

On the other hand there were those who thought that hanging was not a severe enough penalty and were convinced that there would be fewer crimes if it were known that the culprit might be broken on the wheel, whipped to death or hanged in chains alive. Such people fortunately were in a minority and there was no public agitation in favour of more savage punishment.

Title page of Fielding's *Enquiry* (M.DCC.LI = 1751).

AN

ENQUIRY

Into the CAUSES of the late

Increaſe of Robbers, &c.

WITH SOME

PROPOSALS for Remedying this GROWING EVIL.

IN WHICH

The Preſent Reigning VICES are impartially expoſed; and the LAWS that relate to the Proviſion for the POOR, and to the Puniſhment of FELONS are largely and freely examined.

Non jam ſunt mediocres hominum libidines, non humanæ audaciæ ac tolerandæ. Nihil cogitant niſi cædem, niſi incendia, niſi rapinas. CIC. in Catil. 2da.

REQUIEM FOR A MISSING SMUGGLER

From Our Own Correspondent

ROME

There is something touching about he wreaths and carnations dropped into he waters of the Bay of Naples by the :ompanions of a dead smuggler at the ›oint off Capri where he was presumed o have lost his life during a clash with he coastguards. More important is the mplied recognition of respectability for ı profession that the Neapolitans themselves have long accepted as a natural ɔart of life.

From *The Times* of 24 May, 1963.

What was the law?

Stealing goods valued at 40s. from a dwelling house is only one example of many offences which were punishable by death. In spite of increasing wealth, a period of comparative peace, and a large measure of religious toleration, was the law becoming more harsh than it had been in previous centuries? Comparisons are very difficult to make. The law is complicated. No one, however, is likely to be heard arguing that the eighteenth century penal code was lenient. One statute, the Waltham Black Act, is sufficient illustration. Passed in 1722, it remained in force for almost a hundred years and reminds us incidentally that crime was not confined to the big towns and their immediate neighbourhood. Among the offences which this act made punishable with death were: the poaching of game, damage to fish-ponds, the cutting down of trees, maliciously wounding cattle, setting fire to a stack of corn, straw, hay or wood, and trying to get money by means of a threatening letter. And you could hang not only for committing these offences, but also for being with, or afterwards helping, someone who committed them.

No one really knows just how many offences were punishable with death by the end of George II's reign. One authority says 160; but if every variety of each offence is taken into account it is possible to reach the figure 350.

Benefit of Clergy—the right of 'clergy' (anyone who could read) to escape the death sentence—was now of very little use to them, since the words 'without benefit of clergy' were regularly inserted into any act which made new offences punishable with death. The medieval right of Sanctuary—taking refuge in a church or its precincts—was dead too.

However, one medieval institution which did survive was the system of parish constables. The fact that their efforts, combined with those of such honest citizens as were prepared to exert themselves, were the only means of arresting the criminal, gave him or her a good chance of escape.

The word 'police' was only beginning to enter the English language from French during the first half of the eighteenth century and for an efficient police system

A constable.

the country had to wait until 1840. That reform however was initiated by eighteenth century pioneers, one of whom was Henry Fielding.

Bow Street

Fielding was far from taking a sentimental view of his fellow-countrymen, the majority of whom he would probably have called 'People of the lower Sort'. The country's increasing prosperity had put money into the pockets of some of these people; this, Fielding thought, had affected their characters adversely. As he put it 'The Narrowness of their Fortune is changed into Wealth . . . their Humility into Pride, and their Subjection into Equality.' In short, he believed that poor people who became rich tended towards crime; but so did poor people who stayed poor and 'in a very nasty and scandalous Condition'.

> It must be Matter of Astonishment to any Man to reflect that in a Country where the Poor are, beyond all Comparison, more liberally provided for than in any other Part of the habitable Globe [by the Poor Rate levied in every parish], there should be found more Beggars, more distrest and miserable Objects than are to be seen throughout all the States of Europe.

What was to be done? Fielding not only wrote about crime; he dealt constantly with criminals and realized that the great needs of his day were an efficient police force and incorruptible magistrates.

The voluntary Justices of the Peace—often country squires—who were to be found all over England, were often bigoted and ignorant, but it was the paid magistrates of Westminster and Middlesex whose corruptibility had become so notorious that they were known as 'trading justices'. Fielding did not join their number simply out of idealism. He too needed money. But he was content with his salary (£300 a year) and did not augment it by taking bribes. With the job went a house in Bow Street, where the Magistrate lived and the courts were held.

In 1751 Henry Fielding's blind half-brother John became a Westminster magistrate and the two worked together. Henry had begun to organize a force of 'thief-takers' who made more prompt and frequent arrests than the parish constables were able or willing to do. This force, which became known as the Bow St. Runners, was developed by John, who was later knighted and lived till 1780.

Meanwhile Henry Fielding was in grave trouble himself. His health had completely broken down. He was dying.

From the accounts of a Parish Constable near Coventry (1708). He charges for 'returning a warrant' (to a magistrate, probably after making an arrest), for raising the hue and cry (i.e. organizing the pursuit of a criminal), for attending the Christmas, Easter, and Whitsuntide sessions of the justices, for escorting vagabonds, and for mending the penfold (where stray farm animals were kept and claimed). A fine was payable when church bells were not rung on special occasions (e.g. Marlborough's victories), but the entry 'returning the bels', and the fact that no charge was made, remain a mystery.

1708

The disbursments of William Normington Constable of the parish of Anstoy

pd for my oth for the offie —	0	1	0
for my charg —	0	1	6
for returning a warind —	0	1	0
Nov 17 for hur & crye —	0	0	8
My charge at Chrismus sesions	0	1	8
My chargs at Ester Sesions	0	1	8
for returning a warind —	0	1	0
My chargs at whisentit sesion	0	1	8
my chargs for returning the bels	0	0	0
for the conveying the vagabands	0	1	0
for mending the penfold —	0	0	10

CHAPTER VIII

A VOYAGE TO LISBON

'I was now, in the opinion of all men, dying of a complication of disorders.' 'Now' means the winter of 1753-1754. 'I' is Fielding, aged forty-six. Information about his life during those forty-six years is not plentiful. We know much more about Tom Jones and Parson Adams than about their creator—until the closing months of his life. Then, at last, there is a little piece of autobiography—*The journal of a voyage to Lisbon.* This has already been referred to in the section of this book about food (p. 69); but the journal also provides details about disease and its treatment, gives a picture of the trials of an eighteenth century passenger on board ship, and of course helps to complete our picture of Fielding himself.

Diseases and remedies

Fielding was not a hypochondriac. The word must have been known to him. It seems to have come into the English language in the seventeenth century and means a person who thinks he is suffering from all sorts of ailments which are in fact imaginary. Fielding's ailments were not imaginary, but he tried all sorts of cures. His account begins in August 1753, when, as a remedy for gout, he was taking 'The Duke of Portland's medicine'. This was a powder made of dried roots and leaves, which a Duke of Portland had found effective.

Map showing 'Elyng' (Ealing) and 'Kingsington Gravell Place'.

Fielding benefited too, but he must have been suffering from other diseases as well, since in spite of the improvement in his gout, he was advised to go immediately to Bath. Lodgings were booked, but just as he was about to leave London, he was asked to produce a plan to put a stop to gang murders in his district. There had just been five in a week.

Fielding pleaded ill-health, but was persuaded to postpone his journey. In spite of a cold, he produced a plan in four days and received government approval for it. He next contracted jaundice, but stayed at work and succeeded in arresting the leading members of the gang. It was now that his health was 'reduced to the last extremity'; but in the month of December 1753 he had the consolation of knowing that his district was free of street-robberies—an unusual and gratifying state of affairs.

By this time Fielding was no longer considered likely to benefit from the healing waters of Bath. Anyway he was too weak to make the journey. He retired to the country, perhaps to his little farm at Ealing, which he later describes as standing 'in the best air, I believe, in the whole kingdom, and far superior to that of

Kensington Gravel Pits' (a health resort near Notting Hill Gate). In addition to jaundice he was now suffering from asthma, and from a kind of dropsy which gave rise to the accumulation of fluid in the region of the stomach.

No widows' pensions

Why did he work himself to death? Fielding gives a characteristically precise explanation. He felt a duty towards the public and therefore had refused to make a profit from his magistracy. But he was not prepared to kill himself in the public service.

On the other hand his love for his family was limitless and he wanted them to be provided for when he died. Life insurance had begun early in the century, but was not yet common. It is extremely unlikely that Fielding had a policy and there was no system of widows' pensions. His family would depend on the generosity of relations or patrons. So, as he was pretty sure he was going to die anyway, he thought it best to die a hero.

Tapping and tar-water

In February 1754 Fielding returned to London and consulted a successful quack called Joshua Ward. 'Dr.' Ward cut into the swollen stomach and drew off 3½ gallons of fluid. The effect was so weakening that Fielding thought the end really had now come; but he revived and in two months was strong enough to be 'tapped' once more. Meanwhile Dr. Ward had prescribed medicines to induce sweating but these had had no effect and the doctor had said that he might as well have tried to induce sweating in a plank of wood.

The effects of the second tapping were less severe. Fielding attributed this to a dose of 'laudanum', a preparation containing opium. 'It first gave me the most delicious flow of spirits, and afterwards as comfortable a nap.' The suggestion is that the dose was taken *after* the operation. Romans had drugged patients *during* operations but although at this period Roman architecture and poetry were being eagerly studied and copied, their medicine and surgery, like their bathing, road-building, central heating and disposal of sewage, attracted little attention.

During May, after trying a milk diet, Fielding began to take regular doses of tar-water. This was an infusion of tar in cold water—a remedy for dropsy recommended by an Irish Bishop. The result was some increase of appetite, and the next tapping caused less weakness; but the improvement was only slight and hopes now hung not on new remedies but on better weather. Where was this to be found? Not in England, during the summer of 1754. According to Fielding (there were no official meteorological records at that time) the sun 'scarce appeared three times' during the month of May, and the beginning of June was no better. Although thoroughly pessimistic about his condition, Fielding did not want to die before he had to. He therefore decided, after consulting another doctor, to move to a warmer climate.

In search of sunshine

Aix, in southern France, was suggested; but the journey thither by land would have been too exhausting and too expensive. It would have been possible to go by sea to Marseilles, but no ship due to make this voyage could be found in the port of London. On the other hand the great volume of trade between Great Britain and Portugal made it easy to find a ship sailing for Lisbon.

Dr. Doddridge, the nonconformist hymn-writer, had been sent to Lisbon for his health in 1751 (friends subscribed £300 for the journey). He was dead in less than a month from the day he left Falmouth. Nevertheless, Fielding decided to make the journey.

Mails took seven or eight days from Falmouth to Lisbon. By sailing from London, Fielding avoided the long drive to Cornwall, but as things turned out his journey took him fifty days. It began on Wednesday, June 26th, when he was carried on board the *Queen of Portugal* at Rotherhithe. With him were his wife, his eldest daughter with a girl-friend, a manservant and a maidservant.

Merchant ships had no cabins specially for passengers at that time. Like the sailors, most of them had to make do with what space they could find on the lower decks. But a few passengers could be accommodated in the captain's cabin, sleeping on bunks in the tiny 'state-rooms' which adjoined it. Fielding paid £30 to the captain in order to provide this additional comfort for his family.

Eighteenth century merchant ships

Fielding gives no technical details about the *Queen of Portugal*. From Lloyd's Register of Shipping it appears that she was of 130 tons, newly built in America. A number of ships of about this size occur on a list of those using the port of London:

	Tons	Men
Charming Agnes	100	8
Charming Sally	150	14
Duke	130	11
Elizabeth (a very common name)	100	10
Friendship	100	14
Lovely Mary	140	16
Lovely Molly	100	12
Tyger	80	10

Model of a naval dockyard (*c.* 1750).
(*Left*) Small coastal trading vessel carrying supplies.
(*Centre*) One-man treadmill cranes.
(*Right*) A warship under construction.

'Indiamen' were bigger than other merchant ships and those trading with the East Indies were bigger than those trading with the West; they were of about 500 tons by the middle of the century; but this in its turn was small compared with men-of-war, the biggest of which, carrying 100 guns, were of 2,000 tons.

The ship's wheel had begun to replace the whipstaff about the year of Fielding's birth and by the middle of the century it was the usual instrument for steering. Use of the sextant to calculate latitude began in 1731 but an accurate chronometer, necessary for calculating longitude, was not produced till 1761, although Parliament had been offering a reward of £20,000 since 1714. It is interesting that although the British watch and clock industry was flourishing, no one could produce a chronometer, which would not vary more than a second or two per day, until John Harrison, a Yorkshire carpenter, did so and won the prize. 1761 was also the year in which ships' names began to be painted on them.

How to endure a sea-voyage

That a sea voyage may be enjoyed rather than endured by the passengers is a twentieth century idea. Two hundred years ago only chance and temperament could alleviate misery—chance in the shape of a good-tempered captain, a not too unfriendly crew, and winds blowing, but not too stormily, in the right direction. Moll Flanders and her husband were on good terms with their captain when they sailed from Gravesend for Virginia and the relationship was cemented by a present to him of eighty guineas. Furthermore, since they had both just escaped hanging, they were not, for the time being, very hard to please.

John and Charles Wesley, making the same two-month

This wall, built in 1711, still bounds Portsmouth dockyard. You pass under this plaque if you go to visit *H.M.S. Victory* (launched 1765). Notice that both 'the' and 'ye' are used.

voyage (Gravesend-Virginia) in midwinter 1735-1736, faced its problems characteristically:

'We now began to be a little regular. Our common way of living was this: From four in the morning till five, each of us used private prayer. From five to seven we read the Bible together, carefully comparing it (that we might not lean to our own understandings) with the writings of the earliest ages. At seven we breakfasted. At eight were the public prayers. From nine to twelve I usually learned German, and Mr. Delamotte, Greek. My brother writ sermons, and Mr. Ingham instructed the children. At twelve we met to give an account to one another what we had done since our last meeting, and what we designed to do before our next. About one we dined. The time from dinner to four, we spent in reading to those of whom each of us had taken in charge, or in speaking to them severally, as need required. At four were the evening prayers; when either the second lesson was explained, (as it always was in the morning,) or the children were catechised, and instructed before the congregation. From five to six we again used private prayer. From six to seven I read in our cabin to two or three of the passengers, (of whom there were about eighty English on board,) and each of my brethren to a few more in theirs. At seven I joined with the Germans in their public service; while Mr. Ingham was reading between the decks, to as many as desired to hear. At eight we met again, to exhort and instruct one another. Between nine and ten we went to bed, where neither the roaring of the sea, nor the motion of the ship, could take away the refreshing sleep which God gave us.

Fielding's temperament was different from the Wesleys'. He had a sharp tongue and a critical eye at the best of times. Now he was desperately ill. He could not even walk, let alone climb in and out of boats. His face looked so ghastly that pregnant women avoided him for fear of doing some harm to their unborn children. As he was rowed out and carried on board during the afternoon of the 26th June, sailors and watermen jeered. It was an unhappy beginning to what may well have been an unhappy voyage and certainly sounds so in poor jaundiced Fielding's jaundiced account. Here is a summary of the earlier part of the journal:

Thurs., June 27 — Captain in a bad temper. Sailing postponed till Saturday. No reason stated, but he is obviously waiting for more cargo. The tyranny of a captain at sea is as absolute as the tyranny of a stage-coachman over his passengers on land.

Fri., June 28 — My belly needed tapping. Ship's 'surgeon', who was also captain's steward and cook, could not do it, so I summoned Mr. Hunter from London. After the operation I felt much better.

Sun., June 30 — My wife had bad toothache. Sent a servant ashore to bring a tooth-drawer from

Wapping. He found a woman, said to be highly skilled, but before he could get her on board the ship we had begun to move downstream. We are in charge of a pilot while we are in the Thames. He could easily have warned me that we were about to sail, but was too surly to do so. My servant managed to get on board again, but the tooth-drawer would not come with him.

A bright day and much to see—the naval shipyards at Deptford and Woolwich, yachts, Indiamen, ships in the American, African and European trades, colliers, coastal vessels, Thames river craft, and the Royal Hospital at Greenwich. There are very few gentlemen's houses on either bank between Greenwich and Gravesend. Strange, when you think that the much narrower stretch from Chelsea to Shepperton, where there are no big ships to watch, is nevertheless crowded with villas.

But all these splendid sights were spoilt for me by the knowledge that my wife was in such pain. I got a surgeon on board as soon as we reached Gravesend. He advised against extraction and applied opium to the tooth to relieve the pain.

While we were at dinner a coal-smack collided with us. Her bowsprit smashed in through the cabin window. An exchange of the most shocking language between her crew and ours followed.

Mon., July 1st

Still off Gravesend. Two customs officers blundered into our cabin. I knew who they were, because one had broad gold lace on his hat, an ink-horn tied to one of his button-holes and a bundle of papers under his arm. I suggested he should take off his hat. He did so and complained that the mate of the ship should have told him there was a lady and a gentleman below.

About 6.0 p.m. the captain came on

board. (He had travelled by land from Rotherhithe, leaving the ship in charge of the pilot.) Weighed anchor. Pleasant passage downstream; favourable wind and tide; moon just past full.

Tues., July 2nd Off Kent coast. About 3.0 p.m. contrary wind forced us to anchor off Deal. My wife's tooth had become intolerably painful, so I sent for a surgeon. This one tried unsuccessfully to pull the tooth and hurt my wife terribly. She then fell asleep, exhausted. My daughter and her companion were both in their bunks, seasick. The only other passengers were a schoolboy of fourteen and a Portuguese friar who knew no English. So I had to spend the evening over a bowl of punch with the captain. Not very enjoyable. He can only talk about ships and is pretty deaf. I did not want to shout for fear of waking my wife, whose so-called 'state-room' was simply a large-size cupboard opening off the cabin.

Wed., July 3rd No change. At anchor off Deal, my wife dozing, my daughter and her friend sick. Another dull evening with the captain.

Thurs., July 4th Weighed anchor, but could make no progress. Anchored off Deal again. Impossible to go ashore owing to exorbitant price demanded by boatmen (minimum seven shillings and sixpence, rising according to the passenger's degree of desperation. I heard of someone who had been forced to pay 10 guineas for being rowed out to an Indiaman, just before she sailed.)

Sat., July 6th Weighed anchor; again no headway; collided with a sloop when reanchoring off Deal.

Mon., July 8th Set sail 6.0 a.m.; passed Dover; off Dungeness by evening; calm.

Thurs., July 11th After two fine days, hoped to pass south of the Isle of Wight, but a gale forced us

'Careening' was necessary to clear a ship's bottom of weeds and barnacles. Burning off was followed by scraping, after which a mixture of lime, tallow and sulphur was used for repainting.

> to sail up Spithead past Portsmouth [the most important naval dockyard in the kingdom, but Fielding saw little of it, since he could not be on deck during a gale]. Anchored off Ryde.

Shortly before this gale there had occurred an incident which is worth relating in Fielding's own words:

> A most tragical incident fell out this day at sea. While the ship was under sail, but making as will appear no great way, a kitten, one of four of the feline inhabitants of the cabin, fell from the window into the water: an alarm was immediately given to the captain, who was then upon deck, and received it with the utmost concern and many bitter oaths. He immediately gave orders to the steersman in favour of the poor thing, as he called it; the sails were instantly slackened, and all hands, as the phrase is, employed to recover the poor animal. I was, I own, extremely surprised at all this; less indeed at the captain's extreme tenderness than at his conceiving any possibility of success; for if puss had had nine thousand instead of nine lives, I concluded they had been all lost. The boatswain, however, had more sanguine hopes, for, having stripped himself of his jacket, breeches, and shirt, he leaped boldly into the water, and to my great astonishment in a few minutes returned to the ship, bearing the motionless animal in his mouth. Nor was this, I observed, a matter of such great difficulty as it appeared to my ignorance, and possibly may seem to that of my fresh-water reader. The kitten was now exposed to air and sun on the deck, where its life, of which it retained no symptoms, was despaired of by all.
>
> The captain's humanity, if I may so call it, did not so totally destroy his philosophy as to make him yield himself up to affliction on this melancholy occasion. Having felt his loss like a man, he resolved to shew he could bear it like one; and, having declared he had rather have lost a cask of rum or brandy, betook himself to threshing at backgammon with the Portuguese friar, in which innocent amusement they had passed about two-thirds of their time.
>
> But as I have, perhaps, a little too wantonly endeavoured to raise the tender passions of my readers in this narrative, I should think myself unpardonable if I concluded it without

giving them the satisfaction of hearing that the kitten at last recovered, to the great joy of the good captain, but to the great disappointment of some of the sailors, who asserted that the drowning a cat was the very surest way of raising a favourable wind.

From Spithead to the Tagus

Certainly the wait for a favourable wind was long. The ship lay off Ryde till July 23rd. The Fieldings went ashore and lodged with an insufferable Mrs. Francis, who overcharged them. They nearly lost the chest of tea which they had brought with them. When the ship sailed again she soon ran into a storm and for some time the captain did not know where they were; as the weather improved he was relieved to recognize Torbay in Devon. The *Queen of Portugal* lay there from Saturday, 25th, to Thursday, 30th, during which time Fielding threatened to go ashore for good and sue the captain for not allowing reasonable use of the cabin, for which £30 had been paid. (The incident which sparked the matter off was Fielding's refusal to let the captain's servant stow bottles of beer in the cabin while the captain was away and the Fielding family were quietly enjoying their dinner.) Mention of the law terrified the captain and Fielding, whose main wish was to get on with the voyage, forgave him.

On Thursday, 30th July, there was just time for a surgeon to come on board and perform another tapping for dropsy (Mrs. Fielding's tooth seems to have settled down by this time), before a favourable wind sprang up and the ship sailed; but the wind soon changed and the ship had to turn back into Torbay. Not till Saturday, August 1st, did she finally sail out into the Channel and head for the Bay of Biscay, which was reached on Monday, August 3rd. There she was becalmed, struck by a gale, and then becalmed again. On Thursday, August 6th, there was a good N.W. wind; it dropped towards

In *'A Rake's Progress'* Hogarth shows a tailor taking measurements for mourning clothes, while black drapery is nailed to the walls.

evening and the passengers came on deck to watch the sun set in a cloudless sky.

Fair progress was made during the next two days and on Sunday the captain held a small service on deck. Fielding noted the piety of the sailors, who compared very favourably with congregations in London churches, in spite of their uncouth behaviour on other occasions.

On Tuesday, 11th August, they entered the Tagus, a pilot took charge of the ship, an ill-mannered health inspector examined everyone on board and ill-mannered customs officials confiscated all tobacco and snuff, even that for personal use only. Next day, after further wrangling with officials, permission was given for the passengers to land.

SIR,

YOU are desired to Accompany the Corps of Mr. *Thomas Newborough*, from his late Dwelling-House in St. *Paul's* Church-Yard, to the Burial-place of St *Gregory's*, on *Wednesday* the 29*th* of this instant *January*, 170$\frac{4}{5}$ at Five of the Clock in the Afternoon.

A funeral invitation.

There were no more tappings for dropsy. When he had settled into a small house with his family, Fielding's spirits rose sufficiently for him to order new clothes from London (including a wig and 'a new hat large in the brim') and supplies of food from his farm at Ealing (four hams, a hog cut into flitches and a young hog made into pork, salted and pickled in a tub). However, he never wore the new hat, or ate the ham, because he died two months after reaching Lisbon, on 8th October, 1754, at the age of forty-seven.

Funeral expenses

In his last days Fielding may have reflected sardonically that his funeral would be cheaper in a city where he was scarcely known. In London, where he was a person of some importance, his family would have had to bury him in style. When Gay, author of *The Beggar's Opera*, died in 1732, at the age of 43, his body was carried to its burial in Westminster Abbey in a hearse adorned with plumes of white and black feathers, followed by three coaches, each drawn by six horses. Among the chief mourners were a Duke, an Earl, a Viscount, a General and Alexander Pope.

It was usual to present each funeral guest with a 'mourning ring'—a costly trinket—and sometimes a suit of black clothes. Then there was the price of the coffin and the hearse, and everyone expected plenty to eat and drink afterwards. Friends could not be informed, as they usually are today, by an announcement in the newspaper. Invitations had to be designed and printed. Finally everyone, rich or poor, had to be buried in a long flannel shirt, in order to help the wool industry.

It is reasonable to suppose that in Lisbon, where, in addition to having only a small number of friends, the Fieldings had had a struggle to make ends meet, the funeral was a quiet one. About thirty years earlier the British and Dutch communities had bought a burial ground and planted it with cypress trees. (Here Dr. Doddridge had been buried in 1751, at the age of 49.) In a hot country they bury quickly, on the day of death if possible, and towards evening, when the greatest heat is past. This arrangement was well suited to a man of Fielding's impatient spirit. There was no long delay before his shrivelled, yellowing, punctured, six-foot body was lying quietly in what is now called 'The English Cemetery'.

Was Fielding happy?

Doddridge, who lay nearby, had counselled prudence in his hymn 'Ye servants of the Lord':

> Watch! 'tis your Lord's command,
> And while we speak, He's near;
> Mark the first signal of His Hand,
> And ready all appear.

'Fielding', wrote one of his biographers, 'never learned to be prudent.' But the novelist and the nonconformist preacher had much in common. Both hammered away at the British public, both died comparatively young leaving memorable writings behind them. Doddridge's hymns are still sung, and in London at the time of writing a popular film and a popular musical, based on works by Henry Fielding, are running.

Posthumous honours are all very well, but was Fielding happy while he was alive? Lady Mary Wortley Montagu, to whom he had dedicated his first play, thought so. Still a robust correspondent at the age of 66, she wrote to her daughter:

> I am sorry for H. Fielding's death, not only as I shall read no more of his writings, but I believe he lost more than others, as no man enjoyed life more than he did... His happy constitution made him forget everything when he was before a venison pasty, or over a flask of champagne; and I am persuaded he has known more happy moments than any prince upon earth.

We get a somewhat different picture, however, from Arthur Murphy, an actor turned publisher, who brought out the first collected edition of Fielding's works in 1762 and added a wretchedly incomplete biography. He gave it as his opinion that 'our author was unhappy, but not vicious in his nature'.

A golden age?

Generalizations about the man are difficult to make; still more difficult are generalizations about his time—about 'Fielding's England'. After looking at different aspects of it in close-up, as we have done, it comes as a surprise to read of the period of the first two Georges as 'an oasis of tranquillity between two agitated epochs',* considered by some to have been a Golden Age—'the

*Basil Williams, *The Whig Supremacy.*

Hogarth illustrates our free institutions. A newly elected M.P. is chaired (this was supposed to be an honour).

last age of solid, stable, rural England . . . before invention, the machine and the factory made the country industrial instead of mainly agricultural.'*

Finally, it is refreshing to be reminded that in Fielding's day 'foreigners were always asking each other what was the secret of English success, and the answer they found was that the secret lay in our free institutions'.†

* Dorothy George, *England in Transition*.
† G. M. Trevelyan's introduction to *Johnson's England*.

INDEX

Jonathan Swift wrote in 1704:

> The most accomplished way of using books at present is two-fold; either, first, to serve them as some men do lords, learn their titles exactly, and then brag of their acquaintance. Or, secondly, which is indeed the choicer, the profounder, and politer method, to get a thorough insight into the index, by which the whole book is governed and turned, like fishes by the tail. For to enter the palace of learning at the great gate requires an expense of time and forms; therefore men of much haste and little ceremony are content to get in by the back door.

Figures in italics refer to illustrations.

Cock pitt
Bowling Green
Red Lyon Square
High Holborn
Lincolns Inn Square
Oxford Street
St. Giles's
Post House Ground
Covent Garden
Leicester Fields
Piccadilly
St. James's Square
Charring Cross
Savoy
Somerset House
Somerset Staires
Worcester Sta.
Salisbury Sta.
Ivy Bridge
Exchange Sta.
York Staires
Bell Yard
Hungerford Sta.
Brewers Yard
THE
Kings arms Sta.
Whitehall Sta.
Privy Staires
Privy Garden
THE
The Decoy
PARK
Derby Staires
Manchester H.
the Wool Staple
Westminster Sta.
Exchequer
Parliament house
Westminster hall
Parliament Staires
Sungate Sta.
St. Peter's Abby
Peters Street
Market Street
Tuthill
Fields
Horse Ferry
Peterborough H.
Lambeth House
Lambeth
POC
of the
LONDON.W
SOUT
with the
new Bui
Pre